ALSO BY JAMES NELSON

The Trouble with Gumballs

JAMES NELSON

The Poorperson's Guide to
Great Cheap Wines

McGRAW-HILL BOOK COMPANY

New York   St. Louis   San Francisco   Toronto
Düsseldorf   Mexico

1234567890MUMU783210987

3196

Library of Congress Cataloging in Publication Data

Nelson, James Carmer.
The poorperson's guide to great cheap wines,
Bibliography: p.
1. Wine and wine making. I. Title.
TP548.N44   641.2'2   77-7389
ISBN 0-07-046216-X
ISBN 0-07-046215-1 pbk.

For my good friend Warren Ransom,
who introduced me to the enjoyment of wine,
and squandered large amounts of his energy,
money, and native good humor
to acquaint me with many great, un-cheap wines
I might otherwise never have met,
and who also happens to be
my father-in-law.

Contents

Another book about wine?

I wrote this book because I like wine.

I like to drink it, I like to sniff it, I like to look at the light through it and marvel at how beautiful (or clear, or murky, or golden, or ruby red, or whatever) it is.

I like red wines, I like white wines, I like rosé wines. I like apéritif wines before dinner, and table wines with dinner, and dessert wines with dessert. I like sangría in the summer and hot mulled wine in the winter, and I like sangría in the winter and hot mulled wine in the summer, or whenever there's any hot mulled wine around.

However, according to reliable reports (or perhaps unreliable; I can never remember which), there are in print at present some 1,322 books on wine. The world can hardly be said to be holding its breath for yet another book. Why on earth, therefore, would anybody write or publish, or worse yet, *buy* another book about wine?

Well, the book would have to be different from all the others. This book is such a book. It solves an unsolved problem, namely, that the wine the wine lovers love to write about always turns out to be a Château Latour '61 or a Steinberger Riesling Trockenbeerenauslese '59. Marvelous as these wines are, I can barely afford to read about them, let alone drink them. Maybe, if you're reading this book, you're in the same boat. And the other books on inexpensive wines? *Their* problem is that they all seem to think "inexpensive" means a wine that "only" costs $3.50 to $6.00 a bottle.

I grant that most of these books have a chapter on "jug wines," and they nod benignly in the direction of a few California vintners from whom you might expect to get "decent quality in the lower price range." But then they get back to their main topic, which is those $3.50 to $6.00 wines that they consider drinkable by people for whom drinking a $2.99 bottle of wine is dangerously close to slumming.

In doing so, these writers ignore more than 90 percent of all the wine that is consumed in the United States today. They are ignoring vast numbers of new labels that are spreading out from California as a result of the vastly increased planting of wine grapes—mostly of very high quality—that has taken place in recent years. And they are ignoring the enormous influx of new, low-cost wines from Europe, South America, Africa, Australia, and many other wine areas where good harvests and heavy production have put more good, low-cost wines in the market today than have been available to the U.S. consumer in years.

This, therefore, is a book that deals with these wines. Old wines, new wines, undiscovered wines, wines whose prices have plummeted, wines whose prices were low to begin with.

How do you find these bargain wines that you can put on your table for $2.99 a fifth—a fifth of a gallon, that is—or less? How do you know when you've found one? How do you sift out the awful and the ordinary, and come up with high-quality, low-cost wines you'd feel comfortable serving at your Saturday-night dinner party?

This book is designed to help you answer each of these questions. It will tell you where to look for wine bargains, and how to sniff out the stores that offer unusual wine values. It will tell you who to talk to in your area, and what to ask them, and how to get a wine or liquor dealer to run down good, low-cost wines they may not have in their current stock.

It will tell you how to evaluate wines, how to put your eyes, nose, and mouth to work to help you separate the low-cost, sensational wines from the low-cost bummers. And it will tell you how to serve wines so that you get the utmost quality that each wine has to offer.

Finally, it will give you an Index of low-cost wines, all listed by name and recent market price, together with a numerical evaluation of their quality, and a brief paragraph commenting on their outstanding virtues or defects. This is a book that deals with wines named Vinya, Capella, Verdillac, Folonari,

Bodega de Oro, Paisano, Torres, Villa María, and many more.

I have read and enjoyed many books on inexpensive wines, but I have never seen these names or many of the others you will find in the Index of low-cost wines at the back of this book. Until now, no one has taken the time to taste them, evaluate them critically, and write about them.

The principal idea of the book, however, is not to give you a long list of decent, reasonably priced wines from which you can choose at random. The real idea of the book is to show you how to construct your own personal catalog of sound, affordable wines, available where you live, together with suggestions for making sure that your great $1.10-a-fifth Chablis comes off to its best advantage at your Saturday-night supper party.

Using the tools provided in the book, you can not only serve pleasing wines at your dinner parties, but you can discover highly enjoyable, highly affordable wines to wash down the Wednesday tuna casserole or the Thursday leftovers. And you can do it without risking either your palate or your pocketbook. All it takes is some time, a willingness to experiment, a not-very-arduous amount of record-keeping, and an average amount of ingenuity, judgment, and self-confidence.

What's more, you'll have fun doing it. You'll become much more aware of wine wherever you come in contact with it, in your own home, a friend's home, or in a restaurant. In addition, you'll derive a pleasant extra dividend, because in wine experiments, unlike chemistry experiments, you get to drink the results!

I had a lot of fun writing this book, not only because I love wine, but because I also dearly love a bargain. I recently found a Pierre Cardin suit on sale in New York for $39.95. It fitted perfectly, so I bought it, and the whole experience made me feel wonderful.

That same week I also found an extraordinarily pleasant white wine you can serve at your next dinner party—and so can I—at a cost of slightly less than $1 a fifth. That made me feel wonderful, too. And that's what this book is all about.

PART ONE

Great, Cheap Wines

HOW TO FIND THEM,
HOW TO RATE THEM,
HOW TO SERVE THEM.

1

How cheap is cheap?

A friend of mine recently confided over lunch how lucky he felt to have found a case of Château Margaux 1973 for only $16 a bottle. It was a real bargain, and naturally he'd snapped it up, because he knew he'd have to pay twice as much in a year or two.

I had no doubt it was a bargain. It's the same kind of bargain I once heard of from an acquaintance at a cocktail party, who told me that the only truly economical car was the Rolls-Royce. He cited maintenance statistics, depreciation schedules, resale value, and so forth, and actually built a pretty strong case for the fact that a Rolls was a bargain at almost any price.

Despite its bargain status, I still don't have a Rolls, nor have I laid in a supply of those $16 bargain bottles of Château Margaux. And it's not because I don't like bargains. It's just that one person's bargain is another person's major capital investment. You and

I want sound wines on our table, enjoyable wines, affordable wines, wines we're not ashamed to serve to dinner guests. But, we don't want to mortgage our furniture or our children to get them.

In the quest for wines that I could afford, and subsequently, in doing the extraordinarily enjoyable research for this book, I believe I may have tracked down and sampled more different kinds of cheap wine than any person in this country. Red wines, white wines, foreign wines, domestic wines, familiar wines, wines I'd never heard of. But all affordable wines.

Are these wines any good? Take my word for it, some of them are absolutely ghastly. Then there's a big middle group that won't dissolve your gold fillings or corrode the lining of your stomach, but are still very, very ordinary.

Finally, within a very modest price limit, there is a group of wines that are extremely good, some that would be pronounced excellent by experienced, professional wine tasters. Some of these wines, in fact, are the equal of wines selling for $4, $5, or $6 a bottle!

What does "cheap" mean?
So—a word about "cheap." In this book, "cheap" is simply a one-syllable, five-letter way to express the four-syllable, eleven-letter concept "inexpensive." In this book, "cheap" doesn't mean bad, or inferior, or even ordinary. In many cases, in fact, it may mean something quite wonderful. It may, for example, mean a smooth, full-bodied red wine, suitable for serving at your next dinner party, that costs you less than 60 cents a fifth.

It may mean a brilliant, fruity, golden wine that

costs you about $1 a fifth, and has your guests asking, "Hey, what is this? It's *good*!"

In short, it means the great wine *values* of the world, the underrated wines, the undiscovered wines, the underpriced wines, the well-constructed, sound, highly drinkable wines that complement a good dinner and would, if they came out of a bottle with a more aristocratic label, make a devoted wine drinker nod thoughtfully and say, "Very nice. Very, *very* nice."

Fortunately, friend, there are a lot of those wines out there, and you and I are going to find them. But first, let's take a look at what is happening in the world of wine, and how we got to where we are today.

What have *you been drinking?*

We'll start with the fact that, if you're an average American, you've been tossing down 182.5 gallons of *something* every year since you reached adulthood.*
Not just wine, but all the many different kinds of liquids you pour down your gullet.

Back in the year 1953, if you were around then, your tastes were relatively simple. You drank 28.5 gallons of milk each year, 36 gallons of coffee, 7.2 gallons of tea, 3.5 gallons of juice, and 76 gallons of plain old water.

You also had a fondness for soft drinks, but you managed to keep your habit under control and consumed only 12 gallons of Coke, Pepsi, Shasta, or whatever each year.

You didn't drink many alcoholic beverages, but

*According to John C. Maxwell, Jr., the leading industry source for data on consumption trends.

when you did, your preference ran heavily to beer, of which you drank 12.5 gallons, and distilled spirits, of which you drank 1.2 gallons.

You also drank 0.6 gallons of wine, you old devil, you! Your taste in wine ran heavily to the sweeter, higher-alcohol varieties, like Sherry and Muscatel, and unless your family was rich and worldly, or you came from an ethnic background where wine was a customary accompaniment to a meal, you hardly drank any of those funny, not-very-sweet table wines at all.

There is, in fact, a strong feeling that much of the wine consumption of this earlier period was based on the fact that, because there wasn't much demand for wine, it was very cheap. And because it was cheap, a bottle of Muscatel, for example, offered more "proof per penny" than a bottle of whiskey or gin, a fact that had not escaped the notice of the majority of poor alcoholics living along the various skid rows of the nation.

How your tastes changed in twenty years

During the next twenty years, your tastes changed drastically. You still couldn't choke down more than 182.5 gallons of liquid each year, but you began to drink more of this, less of that. By the year 1973, in fact, your consumption of milk had gone down from the 1953 figure of 28.5 gallons to a flat 25 gallons. Your coffee drinking had also gone down slightly from 36 gallons to 35.1, while your use of tea had edged up, from 7.2 gallons to 7.6. Your fondness for juices had climbed appreciably, from 3.5 to 5.3.

Your consumption of soft drinks had zoomed

even more sharply. You now consumed 31.9 gallons a year, compared with 12 in 1953. This may have been one reason why you now drank only 53.5 gallons of water, against 76 gallons twenty years before.

But there were other reasons. On the alcohol beverage front, you were guzzling 20.5 gallons of beer, against 12.5 gallons in 1953, and your intake of distilled spirits had jumped from 1.2 to 1.9 gallons.

And then there was wine. In twenty years you had become so interested in the fruits of the vine that you had nearly tripled your intake. From the 0.6 gallons you put away in 1953, you were now drinking 1.7 gallons. By 1976, you had inched your way up to 1.8 gallons.

In fact, it seemed as though the whole country was suddenly drinking wine. Stockbrokers, kids in college, afternoon bridge groups. Instead of being the drink of the very rich and the very poor, plus a few ethnic minorities, wine had become everybody's drink. And it had become the perfect gift for house-warmings, or for a hurried Christmas present, with the recipient often gauging the strength of the friendship by the name and year on the label.

 Spain, Italy, France: Where they really drink wine!

But even as we watched ourselves knocking back the seemingly incredible quantity of 1.8 gallons of wine per person per year, one look across the ocean told us that, when it came to wine, we were practically teetotalers. Because the average Spaniard drinks 36 gallons a year, the average Italian 39 gallons, and the average Frenchman, lucky dog, 41 gallons. Thus, our country's wine industry—hustling, growing, busting out at the seams—is still outproduced by France, Italy, the Soviet Union, Spain, and Argentina. To wine-bibbing Americans, this is a humbling thought, and many a patriot has made a solemn vow to do his bit to try to help America catch up.

My own discovery of wine parallels the national trend. During the first decade of my life, wine barely existed at all as far as I was concerned, because I was young, and so was prohibition.

During the second decade of my life—the thirties—wine still didn't appear on my personal horizon, except in church. I was an occasional altar boy for the local Episcopal parish, and from time to time I got a faint taste of something unusual on the wafer that was dipped into the chalice just before being deposited on my outstretched tongue. Frankly, it didn't taste very good.

Wine became compulsory during the early part of my third decade, because this was the United States in World War II, and wine was something a sailor had to buy three bottles of in order to earn the right to buy one bottle of a rotgut called Four Feathers. What to do with the unwanted three bottles was always a problem. Someone usually suggested tracking down a sailor with an Italian surname. The only time I ever tried it, it turned out he had the same problem I had. It never occurred to any of us to try drinking it.

Half a dozen years later, however, my wine perceptions underwent a radical change. In the process of marrying my lovely wife, I also married a charming set of parents-in-law, who served no hard liquor in their house. Instead, before dinner, they served chilled Spanish Sherries dry enough to wither your tonsils, while the dinners themselves were often accompanied by bottles of such unfamiliar wonders as Piesporter Goldtröpfchen, Bernkasteler Doktor, Châteauneuf-du-Pape, and Château d'Yquem.

 The author makes a modest discovery about wine
At last, the light bulb went on above my ignorant head. Wine was not just a compulsory purchase to get a bottle of bourbon. Wine was good in itself! It was for drinking! Even before dinner! Even while eating!

Two years after this milestone discovery, my wife and I moved to the Sonoma Valley in California. Suddenly there was wine in profusion. Within a twenty-mile radius there were at least twenty wineries, and believe me, the price was right!

True, there was no Château d'Yquem, but there was an astonishingly good wine that resembled it in many pleasant ways, and cost about one-tenth the price.

True, there was no dry Sherry to compare with my father-in-law's Tío Pepe, but over in the nearby Napa Valley there was a vintner making a Sherry that tasted good even to my father-in-law's discriminating palate. It made him offer the following enthusiastic, if somewhat left-handed compliment, "Why, Jim, this almost tastes like a *real* Sherry!"

Naturally, it costs about a third the price of the fine Spanish Sherries. Even today, it's still an outstanding bargain, representative of the kind of unrecognized values that I plan to talk about in the next few chapters.

The life of a wine drinker is filled with problems
The growing popularity of wine in the United States has not been without its problems. One is how to pronounce all those difficult names, like Cabernet Sauvignon and Pouilly-Fuissé, and another is how not to lose face in a restaurant while trying to decide between a 1969 and a 1965 vintage.

Not to mention the problem of deciding whether it is more chic to have red with meat and white with fish, or to be the kind of person who knows all the rules but conspicuously ignores them.

The wine ceremony; or, customer vs. waiter
Then there is the problem of the wine ceremony, as conducted in an expensive restaurant. This is a stylized drama, not unlike the Japanese tea ceremony, in which a restaurant waiter shows the requested bottle to the customer, uncorks it, offers the cork for the diner's inspection, wipes the mouth of the bottle with extravagant care, and finally, pours a tiny sample into the customer's glass.

The ball is now in the customer's court, and it is up to him to determine whether it is, or is not, fit for his table. It is of no consequence to the ceremony that the customer never rejects a bottle, not even when it tastes like fusel oil. The diner's problem, of course, is that he's totally unsure whether the stuff they've poured into his glass is what he's ordered. His second problem is his belief that the waiter knows everything there is to know about wine, and will sneer, no matter what course of action the diner takes.

True, the waiter may sneer, but chances are his wine knowledge matches that of the legendary diner who, after sniffing and swishing and sipping the sample at some length, turned to the waiter with a bright look of discovery, and said, "Wine! Right?"

It is possible to send a bottle of wine back without suffering ignominy or bodily harm, and everyone should do it at least once during one's lifetime. I did it once, about two years ago, and the incident gave me courage, confidence, and a good story to tell at dinner parties.

 Winesmanship: Nelson & Friedman vs. the Fior d'Italia

It came about through my having lunch—and a bottle of wine—about once a month with my good friend Mike Friedman. We were discussing the apparent boredom with which our waiter had carried out the wine-tasting ritual, when an idea occurred to me.

"Mike," I said, "have you ever sent a bottle of wine back to the cellar?"

"No," he said. "Have you?"

"No," I said. "But I think it's about time."

Then we hatched our plan. The next time we had lunch in our accustomed restaurant, we would reject the bottle, no matter how it tasted.

I could hardly wait for our next luncheon, especially since it was my turn to pay for lunch, which meant that, as host, I would be in charge of the wine tasting.

When the day arrived, I selected a modest California Zinfandel and sat back, waiting for our waiter to run through his act. He uncorked, splashed a few thimblefuls into my glass, and waited.

I sniffed the wine casually, swished it in the glass, took a sip, and tried to look thoughtful. I lifted my eyebrows slightly, ran through a few mouth movements, and took another sip. I paused.

"Mike," I said, "I think you'd better taste this. It seems a bit off to me."

Mike looked properly surprised. "Oh?" he said.

The waiter suddenly came to life. The monotonous pattern of his day had been interrupted. He looked at me, he looked at Mike.

"Give the doctor a taste of the wine, please," I said.

The waiter poured a sample in Mike's glass, and Mike held it up to the light. He swished it around in the glass, sniffed it, and looked at me.

"Hmmm," he said.

He took a sip and looked out over the dining room. He took another sip, rolled it around in his mouth, and put his glass down.

"I see what you mean," he said. "Off. Definitely off. Too acidic. Just not right."

"Better bring another bottle," I told the waiter.

The waiter was dumbfounded. The incident was apparently a first for him, too.

"Another bottle?" he said.

I looked him in the eye. Friendly, cool, James Bond through and through.

"Can't drink this one," I said.

It took some little time for the next bottle to arrive. When it did, it was accompanied not only by our waiter, but by the maître d'.

"I'm sorry about that bottle of wine," he said. "You were right. I tasted it. It was too acid. It happens." He shook his head. "Here, try this bottle."

We repeated the tasting ceremony. Mike and I looked at each other judiciously and nodded.

"This bottle is just fine," I said. The maître d' looked relieved. The waiter still looked stunned.

The maître d' nodded thoughtfully.

"It happens," he said, as he started to move away. "It happens."

I'm sure the kitchen drank and enjoyed our rejected bottle of wine, and I'm sure that, from our continued patronage, the restaurant has recouped its loss. The waiter, though, may never be the same.

 Decisions, decisions! California vs. the United Nations

There are, of course, lots of problems besides the restaurant wine ceremony and the pronunciation of difficult names that face anyone with a growing interest in wine. There is the question of whether to stick to traditional French wines and "be safe," or whether to go exclusively for American wines, or whether to admit both to your cellar (even if your cellar is three bottles stashed in the broom closet). There is the question of whether a wine from Yugoslavia is any good, and even if it is, whether you look like a dummy serving it to company. And so on. In fact, a diligent winesman, playing winesmanship, can find an infinite number of things to worry about.

The problem we're worrying about in this book, however, is *good wines at a price*. If we had unlimited incomes, we'd have no problem finding good wines.

A Bill of Rights for Poorpersons who like wine
But since we don't, we're going to adopt the Poor-person's Magna Carta, which will set down some basic principles from which we will not deviate.

The first article of the Poorperson's Magna Carta is that wine is going to be a pleasure, not a mystique. We are not going to make a religion out of it, nor are we going to use it as a means of snowing our friends (except now and then).

The second article of our Magna Carta is that we're going to drink the wine, not the label. This doesn't mean we won't serve wine in labeled bottles, because sometimes we will, and sometimes we won't. What it does mean is that we're going to judge our wines solely on how they look and taste and smell, and whether they fit within our budgetary limit.

Third, we are going to become detectives and shoppers, not just buyers.

Fourth, and finally, our Poorperson's Magna Carta states that we are not under any circumstances going to drink, serve, or otherwise fool around with any wine we can't put on our table for $2.99 a fifth, or less.

Ours is a pleasant, humanitarian mission. We start it, secure in the knowledge that we can afford it, since most of the world's wine is drunk by people poorer than ourselves, and all but the tiniest fraction of it is cheap. Surely, we are entitled to think of ourselves as explorers, setting out bravely across a vast, uncharted sea of wine, domestic and imported, in search of the Golden Bottle.

2

How to find
great, cheap wines,
AND WHAT TO DO WHEN YOU FIND THEM

You might think that the wine that comes from next door should be cheaper than the wine from thousands of miles away, but that's not always the case. I recently discovered an Algerian red wine that was extraordinarily pleasant, selling for 59 cents a fifth. I discovered it by reading a wine newsletter that ordinarily concerns itself only with very fine, very expensive wines of the kinds that almost never find their way into my home. The writer of the newsletter gave an unusually warm recommendation for the 59-cent wine, because it represented such an outstanding value.

You might think that the bargain Algerian wine was a freak, but this is not so. This kind of bargain will be repeated again and again during the next twelve months. It's up to you and me to track these bargains down, evaluate them to make sure they're really the bargains we hope they are, and, if they are, buy them.

How much do the experts know?

Let me tell you about a wine tasting that took place not too long ago under the auspices of a well-known consumer magazine. First, the magazine assembled a panel of wine experts. Some were professionals who made their living through their wine expertise, and some were private individuals whose cellars and wine knowledge were widely recognized. In a blind tasting—that is, the experts tasted various white wines without any knowledge of which wine was which—the wine that placed fifth, trailing after four lower-priced U.S. wines, was a well-known French wine selling, at the time, for $3.55 for 24 ounces. The wine the experts placed in the number-one spot was an American wine costing $1.25 for a full 25.6-ounce bottle!

Chances are, the experts were red-faced when they discovered what they had done. The lesson for us is that even the trained palates of experts help prove the fact that you don't have to spend a bundle to get a good wine.

So, the first question to be answered is this: Now that you've agreed to pay as much as $2.99 a fifth for a sound, presentable wine, where do you start?

Your liquor dealer can be a big help

Well, your number-one starting place is your friendly neighborhood liquor dealer. Depending on which state you live in, this person may be your supermarket operator, your druggist, a government employee, or simply your friendly neighborhood liquor dealer.

Whichever he or she is, he is a person you want to make friends with, because if he's any good, he can be a big help. Many liquor dealers, particularly those who operate stores with large wine sections, take the trouble to taste their merchandise. Thus, many of them have acquired a knowledge of wine that enables them to give their customers a good bit of fairly expert help. Often, this applies equally whether the customer is wondering which $6.95 Pouilly-Fumé to serve with the fish course, or which of three Burgundies in the $3.50-a-gallon range is the best value.

Taking notes is important

Okay, so you've come to your neighborhood liquor store. Now it's time to go to work. I mentioned earlier that the pursuit of high-quality wines with low price tags involves a modest amount of record keeping, and here's where it starts. Obviously, you have to go about it in your own way, but in case you don't have a way, let me tell you how I do it. I keep a small, thin notebook with me at all times—well, almost all times—and although I occasionally use it for other purposes, I use it principally to record names, prices, and other information about wines that I see on the shelf or taste in a restaurant. Some typical entries might look like this:

> Nov. 29. Don's Liquors: Pedroncelli Sonoma Red. Don recommends as soft, fruity. $3.39 a half-gallon.

Nov. 29. Also at Don's: Villa María Soave. Italian white, nice bottle and label. Don hasn't tried yet. $3.15 for 50 oz.

Dec. 4. Covington Bar & Grill. House red is Sebastiani Burgundy. Velvety, nice bouquet. Waiter says comes in magnums. Should try.

For better or worse, that's the way I keep my "source" record. You'll devise your own way.

Keeping this kind of record also helps you compare prices from one store to another. That's important to a bargain hunter, because even in fair-trade states, not every retailer sells the same wine at the same price. Example: I recently found the same French Muscadet selling for $3.25 in one store and for $2.25 in another!

So there you stand, notebook and pencil in hand, just inside your liquor dealer's front door. You are now ready to start your systematic (and very pleasant) research into the world of great, cheap wines.

Naturally, the first thing you do is to start listing all the wines you see that are bottled in fifths and sell at a shelf price of $2.99 or less. You can list them by winemaker—all the Inglenooks in one list, for example—or you can list them by type, putting all the Burgundies together, all the Zinfandels together, and so on.

Of course, just because you've said you would pay as much as $2.99 a fifth doesn't mean that you're going to start forking out $2.99 right at the start. Actually, you're going to try to beat that figure as much as possible. Nevertheless, you might as well get acquainted with the "top of the line" as far as your particular budget is concerned, and then work your way down to the real bargains.

In my nearby Safeway supermarket, which has a fairly routine department, I recently found 170 different wines that fitted our $2.99-a-fifth budget. That didn't include any "pop" wines or sangrías, nor did it include a very large number of wines in containers larger than a fifth—magnums, half-gallons, gallons, etc.

The incredible variety of wines available

Incidentally, while we're talking about variety, let me point out that in your U.S. wine shop you'll find more different kinds of wines, from more different foreign countries, and from more different regions of the United States, than you will find in wine shops anywhere in the world.

If you lived in Madrid, for example, you would naturally find lots of Spanish wines on the shelves, plus some Port from nearby Portugal, plus a smattering of French wines at very high prices, plus, if you were lucky, a German or Italian wine or two. And that would be it.

If you lived in Paris, you would find a bewildering variety of marvelous French wines, plus a bewildering variety of French wines not quite so marvelous, plus some Spanish wines, and some from Germany and Italy. In a very fashionable shop, you might even find, moldering on the shelves, a lonely bottle of wine from the United States.

The story would be the same in other countries. In an Argentine wine shop recently I found an unlimited quantity of very good Argentine wines, but only a few from Bolivia, a couple from Chile, and that was it. Period. Nothing from Europe, Africa, the United States, or anywhere else.

Where they come from
But let's take the United States. In my Safeway, the one I mentioned just a few paragraphs ago, a store that is not by any person's definition a haven for wine connoisseurs, I recently found wine from Spain, Portugal, Italy, France, Australia, Germany, Japan, Israel, and of course, a large number from the good old U.S.A.

On my way home from Safeway, I stopped in a very fancy, large-volume shop not too far from where I live, and found wines from all the countries I've mentioned so far, plus a substantial representation from Bulgaria, Yugoslavia, the People's Republic of China, Hungary, Greece, Canada, Mexico, Czechoslovakia, Chile, Argentina, South Africa, Denmark, and Morocco!

Many of them, of course, go over our budget. But enough will fall within our limits to make our efforts worthwhile. So, after you're sure your notebook contains a catalog of the store's offering of $2.99-and-under wines, the next thing to do is have a chat with the man or woman who runs the store. Be frank about what you're doing, and you stand a very good chance of enlisting his or her help. This kind of help can often save you both time and money, as well as giving you some ideas about buying wine that may never have occurred to you.

How your dealer can help

You may find, for example, that your liquor dealer has some wines in his back room that haven't yet made it out to the selling floor. If he thinks they fit the specifications of what you're looking for, he'll go into the back room and drag them out. If you've got a particularly tolerant and cooperative dealer, he may even let you look at his price book, containing the printed listing of all the wines available through distributors in his area.

You can't taste a wine that's only a name and a price on the printed page, but if you find one that looks interesting, you can ask your dealer to order some for you, so you can give it a try. Ordinarily, he can't order a single bottle—he has to pay a penalty unless he orders by the case—but if you get him interested in your project, he may turn out to be as curious about the unknown, low-priced wine in the price listings as you are. And if you need a partner in this particular type of research, you couldn't find a better partner than a liquor dealer!

I cannot emphasize too strongly the importance of trying to get a look at the price listings. In California alone, there are some 8,000 different brands of wine for sale, and since many of them come in different sizes, you get a rough total of 10,000 to 15,000 different kinds and sizes of wines available for you to choose from!

No single retailer can carry even a fraction of this bewildering variety. But every retailer in the state can order a case of any wine carried by the wholesalers with whom he deals. So if your friendly neighborhood wine merchant lets you take a peek at his price postings, and if you find a wine from Ithaca or Iceland that you'd like to try, and if you can talk this friendly neighborhood wine merchant into trying to peddle the other eleven bottles, you can try all kinds of wines from all kinds of places at a very modest out-of-pocket cost.

Some store operators know quite a bit about wine and are only too glad to pass their expertise on to a willing listener. Others may never have progressed beyond bourbon-on-the-rocks-with-a-twist. If this is the case with the particular wine merchant who serves your neighborhood, you may as well recognize and accept the fact that you're going to have to find another more wine-oriented dealer.

But don't let that discourage you. Because, even if your first dealer turns out to know quite a bit about wine, you will still want to make a wine safari through a number of other liquor stores. And you'll want to talk to as many knowledgeable wine-oriented store operators as possible, because it's a good idea to get as many informed opinions as you can.

Different stores, different wines

Wisdom is not the only reason for canvassing other stores, however. Wine variety is another. No two stores carry precisely the same wines. This is frequently true even of different stores in the same chain. The variation in wines stocked is often the result of the differing tastes of different neighborhoods, differing tastes of different store managers, and sometimes, as in everything else in life, simple inefficiency and confusion.

So, pencil and notebook in hand, scour the shelves of as many liquor emporiums as your time and patience can stand. Take a Saturday afternoon, or several Saturday afternoons, and visit different areas of your city. Often where you least expect it, you will find a wine you've never heard of before. It may be the store's own "house brand"—wine available only in that store, or chain of stores, and nowhere else. Sometimes, these wines can be very good. Or, it may be a wine from Europe or South America or South Africa, or from a town you've never heard of in California or New York State. But whatever it is, if you haven't seen it before, you'll feel a little like Admiral Peary finding the North Pole.

 Does your town have a Latin Quarter?
If there is a section of your city populated by an ethnic minority accustomed to drink wine, take a look in the liquor stores in that area. Sometimes you'll find a wine or two in these shops that are sold nowhere else in town. Buy a bottle and enter it in your taste-test sweepstakes.

Thus far, I've only talked about those wines that, as they stand on the shelf in their fifth-size bottles, cost $2.99 or less.

 The magic of rebottling
But let's do some mathematics, because the real leverage in putting commendable wines on your table for $1.50 a fifth, or $1.00 a fifth, or $.75 a fifth, or even less, lies in the strategy of buying wine in larger containers and rebottling. Instead of buying a fifth

for, say, $1.49, you buy a gallon for $3.99, and, unless you're giving a party where you're going to use up a whole gallon at once, you put the contents of the gallon into five fifth-size bottles and cork them.

I have in my cellar right now (my cellar is my garage, in case you thought it was something fancier) nine bottles of an extremely pleasant, slightly sweet, slightly fruity Chablis that cost me exactly 64 cents a fifth. The bottles are green and attractive. The labels are suitably home-made. Our guests love it. They can't identify it, and they usually don't ask. My wife and I love it, and frequently find it a more-than-adequate accompaniment to a party dinner, a week-day hamburger, or a pizza from the nearby Straw Hat Pizza emporium.

Here's how I found it. In poking around through a liquor store I had never been in before—notebook in pocket—I came across a Chablis whose name was new to me. The price: $1.89 a half-gallon. You couldn't say the price wasn't right! Of course, I would have preferred to buy a fifth of this wine to take home and try, but it didn't come in fifths. So, I took home a half-gallon and blind-tested it against another good-tasting, somewhat more expensive Chablis of which I was quite fond. I found I liked the new, unfamiliar label, which was the cheaper of the two wines, more than I liked the more familiar, more expensive wine.

For me this was a little bit like Edison inventing the electric light. I was delighted with my find, and, that same evening, so were our next-door neighbors, who came over and helped us finish the half-gallon over meatballs and spaghetti.

The following day, I went back to the store and bought two 1-gallon jugs of this same Chablis. The half-gallon sold for $1.89, the gallon sold for $3.21. I took the two gallons home, rebottled them into ten empty fifth-size bottles I had been saving for just such an occasion. I then laid them carefully on their sides in one of the numerous cardboard wine cartons I use for storage in the garage.

Out of the two 1-gallon jugs I got, naturally, ten fifths of wine. Nine of them are still resting in the bottles I have mentioned. The tenth, as you might have suspected, disappeared the night of the rebottling, along with a succulent dinner of red snapper, broccoli, and fried potatoes.

Now, when a gallon of wine costs $3.21, a bottled fifth of that same wine costs only $.64. Provided, of course, that you, and not the winery, have put it into the fifth-size bottles.

Try it and see. The results will demonstrate that you can really afford to put much better wine on your dinner table than you thought possible, and still stay below—well below—the upper reaches of your budget.

The New Math for wine buffs

Look at it this way. You've already agreed that, for certain especially good wines, you'd be willing to shell out as much as $2.99 a fifth. Well, how many fifths in a gallon? Five. If you multiply $2.99 by five, you get $14.95. That means that you can pay as much as $14.95 for a gallon of wine and, by rebottling, still stay within your $2.99-a-fifth budget.

Don't expect to find many wines selling at $14.95 a gallon, however. The more expensive a wine gets, the less likely it is to come in the gallon size. Nevertheless, a large number of very good wines do come in gallons, half-gallons, and other sizes larger than the standard fifth, and if current trends continue, there will be many more high-quality wines put out in larger containers. With wine consumption increasing, and inflation chipping away at our pocketbooks, more and more people are finding that they don't really want to buy their wine in smallish, costly, 25.6-ounce containers.

So, what do you do if the wine you want to buy at $14.95-or-less per gallon isn't available in gallons? All is not lost. Look for half-gallons, magnums, or 1.5-liter bottles.

Let's talk about half-gallons first. A half-gallon yields 2½ fifths, and 2½ times $2.99 is $7.48. This means you can spend as much as $7.48 for a half-gallon of a wine that pleases your palate, rebottle it into fifths, and still be within your $2.99-a-fifth budget.

A note of caution. If you're rebottling from half-gallons, it's best to buy two half-gallons and bottle them into five fifths, rather than buying a single half-gallon and trying to bottle two full bottles and one half-bottle. If you fill a fifth-size bottle only half full, you'll be leaving too much air in with the wine, and the wine will almost certainly go bad.

Be sure you know your bottle sizes
Now, about magnums and 1.5-liter bottles. Some winemakers are now putting their wines into bottles that look very much like half-gallons but in reality are a size known as a magnum. Other winemakers, as we head toward the metric system, are putting their

wines into 1.5-liter bottles. It's all very confusing, what with wine in fifths, in liters, in magnums, in half-gallons and gallons, in 1.5-liter and 3.0-liter bottles. Not to mention the odd ounce sizes—12, 13, 24, 25, 26, 48, 53 ounces, and so on!

A magnum, incidentally, in case you didn't know, is a bottle containing two-fifths of a gallon of wine. A half-gallon contains 64 ounces of wine, but a magnum contains only 51.2 ounces. Even though the magnum is a time-honored size for many fine French wines, its use by U.S. winemakers has been relatively limited until now. The same is true of the liter-and-a-half container. A 1.5-liter bottle contains 50.7 ounces, about the same as the magnum. In fact, some vintners are now calling their 1.5-liter containers magnums. So, with magnums and 1.5-liter bottles now appearing in front of customers who are accustomed to think that any big bottle is a half-gallon, you should take a careful look at what you're buying, to make sure you're getting the amount of wine you think you are. For a complete list of the new metric bottle sizes, compared with the bottles we've all been accustomed to in the United States, see page 248.

If you can afford to pay up to $2.99 for a fifth, you can afford to pay up to $5.98 for a magnum, and up to $5.92 for a 1.5-liter bottle, and still not violate the articles of the Poorperson's Magna Carta.

The case discount may help

You can even do better than that, thanks to the 10 percent case discount, if you don't mind laying in some inventory. Let me give you an example, just to explain the mathematics.

I'm very fond of Havemeyer Zeller Schwarze Katz, but since it has recently been selling for $3.59 a fifth, it's over my Poorperson's budget. Even if I buy a case of 12 bottles, and therefore get the customary 10 percent case discount, that only brings the bottle price down to $3.23.

This particular wine also comes in magnums, however, at a price of $6.49 per bottle. If I buy a case of six magnums, the case discount brings the price down to $5.84 per bottle. That's clearly under our maximum magnum price of $5.98 for a magnum, and puts me back within the confines of our Magna Carta. So what do I do? I buy the case—I generally have to place a special order with my liquor dealer—and when I get it, I leave three magnums as is, and bottle the other three into six empty fifth bottles. Then I'm ready for any occasion!

Let's sum up all this messy financial information in a table. As long as you buy in the quantities indicated at the top of the table, you can select wines having shelf prices up to the maximums listed in each column and still be putting wine on your table for $2.99 a fifth, or less. Let's take a look:

Allowable shelf price per bottle to stay within Poorperson guidelines

Bottle size	If you buy a single bottle	If you buy a case of 12 bottles	If you buy a case of 6 bottles	If you buy a case of 4 bottles
Fifth (25.6 oz.)	$2.99	$3.32		
1.5-liter (50.7 oz.)	$5.92		$6.57	

Bottle size	*If you buy a single bottle*	*If you buy a case of 12 bottles*	*If you buy a case of 6 bottles*	*If you buy a case of 4 bottles*
Magnum (51.2 oz.)	$5.98		$6.66	
Half-Gallon (64 oz.)	$7.48		$8.31	
3-liter (101.4 oz.)	$11.84			$13.16
Gallon (128 oz.)	$14.95			$16.61

 Supplies for rebottling

So, let's do some rebottling. First, you need empty fifth-size wine bottles, which I'm sure comes as no surprise. You can buy full wine bottles and drink the contents or you can buy new bottles.

You also need corks, which you get in the same way. If you like wine and drink wine, chances are you may have a few empty bottles around the house, and maybe even some corks. In any event, today is the day you stop throwing away corks and empty wine bottles!

If you don't have enough bottles yourself, you can ask neighbors and friends to start saving their empties—and their corks—for you.

If you have a friend in the restaurant business, you might see if there is some way you can get a supply of empties from him. But be careful, because in some states it's against the law for an eating or drinking establishment to do anything other than break empty bottles in which alcoholic beverages of any kind have entered the restaurant.

Finally, of course, when all else fails, you can buy new or used bottles, and new corks. New bottles currently cost about $3.50 a dozen, corks go for about $6.50 per hundred. Once bought, they can be used over and over again—more true of the bottles than the corks, of course, but even a cork can be used two or three times before it's finished.

You'll find a list of suppliers of bottles, corks, labels, and corking machines at the back of the book. Write them for price lists and catalogs. They're well accustomed to handling mail orders.

Okay, so now you have a big collection of empty wine fifths, and some corks, new or otherwise, and some gallon bottles of a fine Sauterne or Burgundy or Zinfandel that you want to put into the fifths.

Why rebottle? Spoilage is one reason
Maybe, as you start the process, you're wondering why you're rebottling at all. Why not just open up the gallon, use what you want, recap it, and put it away for another day?

The answer, of course, is that the large amount of air in the partially emptied gallon bottle will cause the wine to deteriorate. Then, next time you invite your friends over for dinner, the wine won't taste half as good as it did when it was first opened. By rebottling, you can open a small amount at a time, while the rest sits safe, fresh, and we hope, cool, in your cellar, garage, closet, or basement.

Rebottling: Psychology is another reason
Another reason for rebottling, which really belongs in
the chapter on serving wines, is that the effect of
opening a fifth and putting it on the table at dinner is
quite different from the effect you get by plunking a
gallon jug on the table.

Even if a gallon is freshly opened, and your party
is going to empty it before the evening is over, there's
something psychologically more pleasing about pouring from a nice, green, unlabeled or home-labeled
fifth than from a gallon-size container. It's a little like
the difference between having a single, beautiful
ruddy apple served to you on a china plate, with
appropriate silverware and a napkin, or taking the
same apple out of a bulky paper sack.

Same apple, different experience. Same wine, but
it doesn't *seem* the same!

The first thing you want to do before rebottling is
to wash the bottles inside and out. If you're fussy or if
you're planning to store the wine for a year or more,
you may want to sterilize them. If you don't know
how to wash and rinse a bottle, I'm not going to help
you, but you may need help on how to sterilize one. All
you do is wash the bottles and put them in the
oven—make sure the oven is cold—and then heat the
oven to about 450 degrees. Let the bottles "bake" for
an hour or so; then turn the oven off and let them cool
down. When it's all over, you will have some nice,
clean bottles that are free of any yeasts, bacteria, or
other adulterants that might cause some change in the
wine you're going to store.

Now, the corks. As we mentioned earlier, they
can be new, or they can come from previous bottles of

wine you may have opened. If they're used, but in pretty good shape, considering what you did to them with the corkscrew, then they'll do for rebottling. If you mangled them excessively in getting them out of the bottle, you might as well toss them out.

At this point let me put in a plug for the "Ah-So" opener. It's an unusual device that has two flat legs that you insert on either side of the cork, between the cork and the bottle. Once the legs are inserted, you twist the opener and pull, and out comes the cork, completely unpunctured, unharmed, and ready to go again. I like it better than any corkscrew I've ever used. It's easy to use, and it's ideal for budget-minded wine drinkers who want to get the maximum mileage out of every cork.

Using a clean funnel, fill your five bottles. If the gallon doesn't quite seem to stretch, fill four bottles to within half an inch of the cork, and let the fifth bottle fill as much as it can. If it falls short of the half-inch-from-the-cork mark, don't worry. At least you've confined your air-deterioration problem, if any, to a single bottle, rather than spreading it evenly over all five bottles. Drink the slightly short bottle soon, with the Wednesday hash perhaps, and save the other four for nobler occasions.

Corking bottles

We now come to the problem of corking the five bottles. There are two ways to accomplish this: (1) brute force; (2) a corking machine.

Which of these two methods you use is up to you. I used the brute force method for quite a while, accompanying it with grunts, groans, and various expletives. Subsequently, I bought a hand-held corking machine for about $9.00 and have been happy ever since. You can get a simple two-stage corking machine (the first stage is compressing the cork, the second driving it into the neck of the bottle), for prices ranging from $7.98 to $70.00 from various of the equipment sources listed in the back of the book. In my book, they're worth it.

Either way, brute force or machine, you should soften the corks in warm water before you try putting them into the bottles. Some counselors advise you to boil them before putting them in. Others say that boiling destroys significant amounts of cellulose in the cork. However, since we are not laying down a Château Latour to mature some twenty years down the road, but rather are simply trying to assemble a small, drinkable cellar without going to debtor's prison, we need not be quite as fussy about our techniques as the château bottlers. Be clean, be careful, but don't turn it into a religion.

Now that you know how to rebottle from gallons to fifths, let's get back to the business of how to find wines worthy of rebottling. Let's see how many ways there are for finding sound, enjoyable wines, and getting them at the right price.

House wines can aid your search

Well, one thing to consider is the fact that almost every restaurant nowadays has a "house wine." In fact, since wine prices have skyrocketed, many *bon vivants* who always used to call for the wine list and spend twenty minutes deciding whether to have a Cabernet or a Pinot Noir now simply ask for a carafe of the house red. They frequently get a pretty good wine in the bargain.

For the bargain hunter, a restaurant's house wine is simply another chance to evaluate a wine that you can probably afford to put on your own table. Even restaurants with very high standards are now serving house wines poured from larger-than-fifth-size containers, wines that cost less than our top allowable prices. So, next time you have a restaurant meal, have a glass of the house red or the house white along with it. If you enjoy the wine, ask the waiter about the brand and type. If the waiter leaves you wondering whether or not he got the answer to the question right, go to the bar and ask the bartender on your way out. In almost every case, provided it appears that you're asking the question because you enjoyed the wine, you'll find the bartender happy to haul out the bottle from which he poured your glass and let you have a look at the label.

Then, out with the notebook. Write it down: the type of wine, the maker, any special information on the label, the name of the restaurant, and the date. Also write down anything else that you thought significant about your enjoyment of that particular glass of wine.

For example, did they fill your glass at the table from a carafe? If it was a white wine, did they supply you with a chilled glass? Was there anything special about the glass itself—its design, color, ornamentation? And so forth.

Through ordering house wines and asking questions later, I have found a number of wines of which I think very highly. I now regularly decant these wines from gallons and half-gallons into fifths, cork them, and lay them down in my garage-cellar. At the same time, from dining in an expensive restaurant and watching an experienced, knowledgeable waiter serve half a liter of house wine, I have confirmed over and over again my long-time belief that the enjoyment of a good glass of wine is only about 50 percent dependent on the wine itself.

 Wine tastings
How else to find good wines? Go to wine tastings. If you happen upon a wine you like especially, find out if it's available in the larger sizes. Even if it isn't, write it down in your notebook. When your ship comes in, you may be willing to pay a good bit more than $2.99 a fifth for your table wine.

 Winery towns
If you live near wine country, go visit the wineries. Visit the big ones, and visit the small ones. Taste everything in sight. Ask questions about sizes and prices, and be sure to ask about any wines that are available only at the winery. The Louis M. Martini winery in St. Helena, California, for example, makes an excellent dry Sherry that used to be available at the winery in gallons, but through liquor outlets only in fifths. Alas, Martini gave up that practice some time back, and fifths are now the only size available. The winery is still the only place you can buy Martini's

delicious Moscato Amabile, a lovely white dessert wine, but alas again, it doesn't fit our Poorperson's budget. Why do I give you this example of a size that's discontinued and a wine we can't afford? For the principle of the thing—so you'll remember, when you take a wine tour, to ask about special wines and special sizes available at the winery, and nowhere else.

Pricing in fair-trade states

People who live in states without "fair-trade" laws will undoubtedly feel a swell of compassion toward those unfortunates who live in states that have them. Fair-trade laws, in case you're not familiar with them, are statutes that give manufacturers, and in some cases wholesalers, the right to set a price below which it is against the law to sell their products at retail.

The fair-trade laws came into being during the Depression of the 1930s, ostensibly to protect the small retailer from the price onslaught of the big chains. While this was a commendable objective, it has been argued that, at present, the fair-trade laws simply provide a convenient mechanism for price fixing, and for frustrating the noble principle that the price of a product is a function of supply and demand.

If you live in a state without fair-trade laws, nobody has to tell you that you can save money by shopping around. When retailers are free to set the prices of their goods, you frequently find wide variations in prices for identical products. Naturally, what's true for electric razors and Sony television sets is also true for wine. In states without fair-trade laws, therefore, it pays to read the ads, watch for bargains, and check shelf prices of the wines you want to buy, before you buy them.

You'll also occasionally find in non-fair-trade states that you can "deal" with the store operator. Thus, if your individual order is big enough, or if business is bad enough, or if you can get a bunch of friends to pool orders so that your business is of unusual significance to a dealer, you can often buy your wines at savings even greater than those of the advertised specials.

Even in fair-trade states, however, there are bargains. Retailing being what it is, when a product doesn't move, you have to have a clearance sale. In a fair-trade situation, this often doesn't look like a clearance sale, in that the price cut may not be advertised, and the store may not have a bargain basement. So, you've got to look, and you've got to ask.

As an example of what can happen, let me tell you the story of a fine French wine with a long name that got a big promotional push about a year ago. The wine, a high-quality white, was advertised as the perfect complement for fish dishes, and a good bit of money was spent trying to promote its popularity.

Unfortunately (fortunately, say the bargain hunters!), the campaign laid an egg. The wholesaler, who had posted a minimum resale price in the $3.25-per-fifth range, finally got tired of carrying the inventory. A big retail dealer with several stores offered to take the inventory off his hands at a very low figure. The wholesaler agreed.

The wholesaler then posted a new minimum

resale price with the state Alcohol Beverage Control Commission, and suddenly it was legal to sell this $3.25 wine for $1.49 a bottle, which the big retailer proceeded to do. For such a fine wine, the price was ridiculously low, but that's the force of circumstance. And that's what keeps us bargain hunters on our toes.

Outside the law

There is another kind of bargain in a fair-trade state, and unfortunately it's slightly illegal. I do not want to encourage anyone to disobey the law, but at the same time it would only be telling part of the story if I didn't let you know that there is a substantial volume of price-controlled liquor and wine that moves regularly through retail channels at prices well below the official fair-trade prices. These dealers—known in California as "bombers"—probably do four times the volume in half the floor space occupied by their legitimate brothers operating two blocks up the street, simply by selling their merchandise at 10 to 30 percent below the prices the wine and liquor companies post with the state.

I won't tell you how to locate these stores, because what they do is against the law. And anyhow, your Uncle Al or your cousin Fran or the couple who lives next door know a lot more than I about which stores are doing it in your town.

By now your notebook should be brimming over with useful information. You have long lists of wines that fit within the $2.99-a-fifth limit we've put on your expenditures, both those that cost $2.99 or less when sold in fifth-size bottles, and those that qualify when you buy the larger sizes and rebottle. You have names of house wines from your favorite restaurants, and the recommendations of wine dealers and bartenders and knowledgeable friends.

So now the problem changes. It becomes: Which of these many wines should you buy?

 You *are the final judge*

Actually, the answer is up to you. Because in the final analysis, you are the person who is going to drink the wine. You are the person who is going to serve it to your guests. And, let's not forget, you are the person who is going to pay for it. Therefore, you're the person who, aided by whatever judgmental mechanisms we can come up with to help you, has to make the final purchase decision.

Actually, it isn't all that hard. And as I mentioned before, it's fun. In the next chapter I'll tell you how to go about it.

3

*Evaluating
what you find*

"It's cheap, but is it good?"

Once, during the time that my wife and I lived in the wine country of California, we gave a party built around our guests' sense of taste, smell, and touch.

Each guest was given a pencil and paper and was then conducted individually through a series of tests designed to give him an idea of how discriminating or undiscriminating his senses were. We didn't fool around with sight or hearing, because we use these senses so actively and so often that they're usually pretty well honed. Our other senses, however, don't get this same vigorous daily workout.

For the touch test, each guest was given ten small fabric bags, each containing a different familiar article, such as a paper clip, a clothespin, a rubber eraser, and so forth, and securely closed with a tied drawstring. The object was for the guest to identify the item in the bag, simply by feeling it with his hands. Our guests did pretty well on the touch test.

The smell test consisted of uncorking and sniffing the contents of ten different bottles, and then writing down the identity of the item sniffed. Again the smells were all familiar, everyday smells—rubbing alcohol, wintergreen, vanilla extract, ammonia, bourbon whiskey, and the like.

Our guests didn't do as well on the smell tests as they did on the touch test, but they still did fairly well.

The items in the third test—taste—included milk, Coca-Cola, bicarbonate of soda, plain water, tea, coffee, and four other items. We blindfolded our guests so they wouldn't get any visual clues and served them the ten different drinks, one at a time, letting them taste each one as many times as they wanted. Also, to eliminate clues that had nothing to do with taste (coffee is hot, Coke is cold and carbonated, etc.), we served each beverage at room temperature, and in the case of soft drinks, let the fizz disappear.

How did our guests do on this test? They went bananas. They tasted milk and swore it was bicarbonate of soda. They tasted Coca-Cola and called it tea. They made positive identifications and doubtful identifications, but for the most part they made outrageously wrong identifications.

They couldn't believe it. Neither could we. It seemed that nobody could do as badly as almost everyone had, and yet the evidence was unmistakable. People who had sworn they could tell Coke from Pepsi blindfolded could barely tell it from ginger ale. We moved on to dinner and discussed the shameful results over many bottles of good, cheap, Sonoma County wine.

For our present investigation, the fact that emerges from this simple-minded party game is that, almost without exception, taste is everyone's least reliable sense. Furthermore, second place in the unreliability sweepstakes goes to our sense of smell. When you stop and think that taste and smell are what everyone uses in deciding whether a wine is a great wine or an absolute dog, you'll begin to realize that very few people know very much for certain about wines, or how to evaluate them.

In this chapter, therefore, you're going to learn something about how to sharpen up your taste buds, and how to discipline your sense of smell. And you're going to learn how to compare one wine with another in a way that, if not exactly scientific, is at least logical, and likely to produce results that you can live with happily ever after, and maybe be extremely proud of.

The first step in the process is an easy one. You simply stand in front of a mirror, look yourself in the eye, lift your chin, straighten your shoulders, and say, "Never again will I underestimate the ability of my precious taste buds. And that goes for my nose, too."

If you need encouragement in thinking that your nose and taste buds are as good as anyone else's, consider the great French Wine Scandal of 1974.

Mon Dieu! Trouble in the French wine trade!
The scandal erupted in the Bordeaux area of France, a district from which come some of the world's finest,

most famous, and not surprisingly, most expensive wines. The French government levied charges against some of the most prestigious winemakers and shippers, charges that included the most heinous crimes known to dedicated wine drinkers, far outstripping murder, rape, and plunder.

It was alleged, for example, that the Bordeaux vintners had promoted some of their wines from buck private to brigadier general simply by falsifying a few legal papers. A few quick strokes of the pen, and cheap red wines from the south of France became members of the Bordeaux nobility, bearing cherished names and price tags to match. Other wines, so poor that they were fit only to be made into vinegar, were "recovered" through treatment with chemicals, and were then sold for fancy prices.

Still others, it was alleged, were upgraded simply by switching the labels. And some costly Bordeaux reds that were in very short supply suddenly became plentiful through the judicious and totally surreptitious addition of less costly white wine.

Many of these wines were then, predictably, shipped to the United States.

The real scandal, according to one American wine connoisseur who commented on the affair, was that nobody, including the experts, seemed to have noticed the difference. The villains went merrily on, adulterating, switching labels, and in general making silk purses out of sows' ears. The wine bibbers, or at least those sophisticated enough to want the wines in question and well-heeled enough to afford them, tipped back their glasses and drank to one another's health, completely unaware that their joy was counterfeit.

"Wine experts?" said one American connoisseur. "About all that most wine experts can tell about a wine is whether it's good or bad, whether it has turned vinegary or smells skunky."

Another renowned U.S. wine pundit agreed heartily that most experts can't really tell the difference between a tampered wine and the real thing. "Even if the wine was authentic Bordeaux, there are many variables involved. The taste of a wine can change from bottle to bottle in the same case. The light in the room, the glass from which it is drunk, the cork, all have an effect."

The best thing to do, he concluded, was to relax and enjoy the wine, whatever the label might say.

If the experts are confused, where does that leave you and me? Well, it leaves us dependent on our own palates, our own noses, our own taste buds. Actually, that's not a bad dependence, because the kind of wine we want to drink and serve to our friends is the kind of wine that tastes good to *us*, and not necessarily what appeals to those people generally referred to as "the experts."

This is not to put the experts down. We need experts, and they are not dummies. Without people who care about the quality of wine, there would be no wine, because the first expert needed in the wine equation is the winemaker himself.

We need the wine connoisseurs and critics, too. They, because of their long experience and exceptional sensitivity to smells and tastes, can offer the rest of us some general guidelines that will help us evaluate wines and separate the good from the bad. They can even help us separate the very, very fine from the just plain good.

You, and only you, know what you like
What they can't tell us, however, is what we like and what we don't like. After all, there's no expert in the world who can give an authoritative pronouncement on whether chocolate tastes better than vanilla. You wouldn't believe him if he did, because it's an individual judgment. In other words, the final judgment on matters of taste preference is completely and totally up to you.

So, let's start evaluating some wines.

Let's say you've gone out on a wine-collecting mission, and you now have three or four fifths of different white wines that fall within our price guidelines. Now you want to check them out to see whether to buy some more of them—say, for example, buy some gallon containers and then rebottle—or strike them off your list and avoid them forevermore.

The best way to judge these wines—or any wines, for that matter—is to judge them in a side-by-side comparison. In other words, the most effective way to judge a wine is to compare it with other similar wines, and not to judge it all by its lonesome.

The remembrance of things past
If your eyes, nose, and mouth have a rough equivalent of that rare quality of the ear known as perfect pitch, then side-by-side comparison probably isn't all that important to you. Perfect pitch is really nothing more than perfect memory of a previously heard sound that has been adopted as a standard against which to measure other sounds.

Thus, if your eyes can remember the visual

qualities, good and bad, of the wines you tasted yesterday and last week and last year, and if your nose and mouth can do the same thing for the wonderful smells and tastes of wines you've consumed in your checkered past, then your wine evaluation standards are more or less built-in.

The rest of us, unfortunately, don't have it that easy. We find it hard to remember smells precisely. Our taste buds shrug and look the other way when asked to recall a complex taste experience from the past. Sure, we have pleasant memories of a good dinner, an exotic perfume, an enjoyable bottle of wine, but our recollections are usually general, not specific enough to serve as reliable standards against which to measure the various merits and demerits of a new, untested bottle of wine.

Side-by-side testing

The moral is: Whenever possible, test two, three, four, five, or more similar wines on a side-by-side basis. As you do more and more evaluations, you will probably find that you have a few favorite wines that become standards. Thus, if you are going to evaluate three new white wines, toss in your "standard" white as a reference point. That way, when you're through judging, you'll know whether each of the other three is, in your opinion, better or worse than the wine you have designated as your standard in that category. You may even find that such a comparison will persuade you to make a different wine your standard.

Before you can judge the merits of four or five wines, however, you need to know how to judge just a single bottle. You need to know what to look for in terms of sight, smell, taste, and mouth-feel. You need to know how to consider the various aspects of a wine one at a time, and then again as an integrated whole. And you need to know some words to help you describe your perceptions, so you can write something useful in your wine log.

So, let's open just one of your bottles of white wine. Since it's white, it should be cold. How cold? About as cold as wine gets after two or three hours in the refrigerator. (Not in the freezer, of course.) The first step, of course, is to uncork your bottle. The word "uncork" may not be totally accurate, because the bottle you're going to evaluate may have come with a metal screw-type closure. For many years, I used to think that this kind of metal closure was somehow technically inferior to a cork, but this is not the case. True, you'll generally find metal closures on bottles of lower-priced wines, and corks in the necks of the more expensive ones, but that's not necessarily related to their abilities to preserve wine over a long period.

 Air is the enemy
Both closures keep wine's old enemy, air, from getting into the bottle and spoiling the wine. The metal closure keeps air out, period. The cork closure, some winemakers feel, allows the wine to breathe a bit, permitting, over the many years that a wine may lie aging on its side in a cool cellar, imperceptible amounts of air to pass through the wine-soaked cork

(in which direction I'm not sure) for the ultimate greater glory of the wine when it is drunk.

Whether this is the absolute truth or a wine-maker's fairy tale, I don't know. What I do know is that there is a great deal more ceremony, drama, and pleasant tribal ritual in withdrawing a single purpled cork from the neck of a bottle than there is in unscrewing fifteen patented metal closures.

Sniffing corks

Got your bottle open? Okay, if you opened it by withdrawing a cork, you might as well sniff the wet end of the cork to see if it gives you any clues. Actually, it will only give you clues of the grossest type. For example, if the end that's supposed to be wet is dry and crumbly instead, this could mean that the bottle has been stored standing up rather than lying down. The result is that the cork has dried out, and when the cork dries out, the air gets in, and there goes the neighborhood.

On the other hand, if the cork is nice and moist, it probably means that the wine has been properly stored on its side. A moist cork is no guarantee that the wine hasn't turned to vinegar, but if it has, you'll probably get a vinegary whiff from the cork.

If you don't get any whiff at all, don't worry. Neither do a lot of other people who sniff corks. So sniff it, pause, look suitably thoughtful, and then put the cork down beside the bottle. The great wine ritual has begun, and you've already scored two points for corksmanship.

Choosing glasses

Now, pour some wine into a glass. What kind of glass? Well, you can taste wine in a cut-crystal tumbler or a plastic orange-juice glass. However, since the way you serve wine can affect the way you perceive the wine's quality, you might as well give your wine the best possible chance to succeed, by serving it in a fair-sized, simple, clear, slightly tapered wineglass with a stem. By fair-sized I mean a glass that will hold about 10 ounces if filled to the brim, although you naturally won't ever fill it that full. Fill your glass about a quarter full. You are now about to go through the kind of scoring procedure that the professors of viticulture and enology—grape growing and winemaking—use at the University of California at Davis.

 The University of California scoring system

These professors are renowned for their wine expertise and use a scoring system that looks complex at the outset. Actually, after you've worked with it for a while, it's not that hard at all. It's only one system of several you can use (we'll talk about another one later), but it's a good one, because it breaks the wine experience down into its individual component parts. Long term, you may find you'd rather use a simpler system for your judging, but you'll also find that a short-term use of the University of California system will acquaint you with each of the various basic wine characteristics the professors and critics and connoisseurs think are important.

The system rates wines on ten separate characteristics, and assigns points for each. Here are the categories and the maximum number of points allowed:

Characteristics:	Maximum points:
Appearance	2
Color	2
Aroma and bouquet	4
Acescence	2
Total acid	2
Sugar	1
Body	1
Flavor	2
Astringency	2
General quality	2

We'll take up each characteristic one at a time. But in the meantime, you should know that the system uses a scorecard, and if you want to use this system, you will, too. It doesn't matter whether you record your scores in a loose-leaf notebook or a file of 3 x 5 cards. The main thing is to establish a written, dated record of how you rate various wines on the scale from zero to 20.

A perfect wine, if there is such a thing, would score a full 20 points in the U.C. system. A wine that scores zero would undoubtedly clean the rust out of your car radiator.

For a sample of what your scorecard should look like, more or less, take a look at page 62.

Okay, your glass is now about a quarter full of an unevaluated white wine, and you're ready to begin. So, let's judge the wine on the first characteristic: appearance.

Appearance: 2 points

Hold the glass up to the light and take a look. You'll need good light and a white background in order to get a really good look at the wine. If your kitchen, dining room, or parlor doesn't happen to have a white background, you can always hang up a sheet, a tablecloth, or a big swatch of white shelf paper.

Does the wine look clear? Is it cloudy? Or is it somewhere in between? If there is no sign of any suspended material floating around in it (pieces of cork don't count), and if it has a nice, sparkling, clear look to it, you can say that the wine is *brilliant* and give it 2 points. Two points is the most a wine can earn for its appearance.

If the wine has a slight haziness, but not enough to cause you to notice it the first instant you look, you call it *clear* and give it 1 point. If you notice the haziness right away, however, you call the wine *dull*, and if it's worse than just hazy, and has quite a bit of suspended material, you call the wine *cloudy*. In either case, dull or cloudy, you score your wine with a big fat goose egg in the appearance category.

Does that sound difficult? If it does, I've misled you, because all it means is this: Is the wine nice and clear (2 points)? Or is it cloudy (zero)? If you can't make up your mind whether it's clear or cloudy, give it 1 point, and move on to the next scoring category, which is color.

 Color: 2 points

If you're judging a $7 bottle of Bernkasteler Doktor, the color may give you some problems. The reason is, some people have been drinking and judging this famous German white wine for years and years, and they know what it "ought to look like." Fortunately, this is unlikely to be a problem for us. All we really need to decide, therefore, is whether the color is pleasing to our eye, and whether, in some only slightly definable way, it's matched to the taste of the wine.

The color range of white wines runs from light straw yellow, which is the lightest shade of the lightest wines, such as Chablis, through medium yellow, light gold (we're getting darker now), and on into light, medium, and dark amber.

Judging the color of whites

If the white wine you are judging, therefore, has a pleasing color, principally yellow, gold, or straw (amber is for Sherries, Ports, Muscatels, and the like), give it the full 2 points. If it's bleached looking, almost colorless, give it 1 point or none. Nobody likes a watery-looking (or -tasting) wine. You can also give it 1 point or none if it looks brownish, or has any other unpleasant color overtones. If a white wine looks a tiny bit green, don't worry. In fact, you can even feel slightly good about it, because it may just be residual chlorophyll, which in many cases is a desirable characteristic.

Portugal is famous for its *vinhos verdes*, or green wines, which are called green because they are made from grapes that have not fully matured. Sometimes they have a greenish cast, although not always, and to round out their theme of greenness, they are drunk very young. California has its green wines, too, and they generally score a solid 2 points on the rating scale.

Judging the color of reds
Red wines range from low pink, which means washed out, through medium pink, low red, and medium red, to high red. Medium pink is what most rosé wines are supposed to be, and medium red is the standard for the great bulk of red wines. So, if you've bought a bottle of wine that's labeled Burgundy or Claret or Zinfandel, it ought to be a nice, rich, red color and you should score it 2 points. If it has a few hints of purple, you're into what is known as the high red area, and there's still no need to knock off any points. On the other hand, if your Burgundy is pink instead of red, better give it 1 point, or none, depending on how light the color is. Naturally, it's the other way around for rosé wines. If they're too red, you'll want to knock off a point or two. Same thing goes in case they're "watery pink." Don't worry about whether or not you're doing it right. You'll develop a feeling for color after you've looked at a number of wines—*really* looked, that is, which is something you may not have done much—and swirled them in a glass and held them up to a good light.

Aroma and bouquet: 4 points
We now move on to aroma and bouquet, a category otherwise known as "Does it smell good?" Since smell is such an important part of the wine evaluation process, your wine has an opportunity to score 4

points for this characteristic. This is more points than we award for any other single characteristic.

Swirl the wine in your glass. This gives it a chance to "breathe," and to release its fragrance. It also gives you a chance to ponder the difference between aroma and bouquet, which are really not the same thing.

If this news surprises you, don't be concerned, because the difference is not really that important. Still, as a budding wine bore, you ought to know.

Judging aroma . . .

Aroma is that odor which comes from the fact that what you are smelling is, in actual fact, the juice of crushed grapes. The experts describe this grapey smell as the wine's aroma. If the wine smells nice and grapey, but not like any specific variety of grape, you describe the aroma of the wine as being *vinous*.

If you are knowledgeable enough to be able to smell a wine and detect that it is indeed made from a particular variety of grape, then, even if you can't identify the variety, you call the aroma *distinct*. If you can actually identify the grape as a Zinfandel or a Cabernet or a Pinot Noir, you go to the head of the class and announce that the aroma is *varietal*. Naturally, in assessing aroma, the intensity of the aroma gets evaluated, too. It can be light, medium, or high, and as you might already have guessed, high is best.

. . . and bouquet

Now we come to bouquet. Bouquet is a product of the aging of wines. It is what happens after the wine is put into the barrel, or subsequently, the bottle, and it has to do with the reaction between its alcohols and acids.

It often results in a somewhat sweet, fruity, unusually pleasant smell. To some noses a wine may have a bouquet that makes them think of violets, or clover, or roses, or any of a number of other agreeable smells. When such a bouquet is strong, you'll find you can get a lot of pleasure from just sitting and sniffing, long before you take your first taste. Just remember, however, if you want to be precise in describing this smell, not to call it aroma, because it isn't. It's bouquet.

How should you score your wine on aroma and bouquet? Well, some professional judges say that, as a starter, they give a wine 2 points if it smells pleasantly vinous, 3 if it has some varietal overtones, and 4, if it has a nice, recognizable varietal aroma. At the same time, since aroma and bouquet share the same four points, the judges admit that they are mixing their perceptions of bouquet in with their perceptions of aroma and at the same time are scoring the intensity of both these factors. How they make this extraordinary computation is their own mysterious secret. How *you* make it is yours.

 In simpler terms . . .

My own way is to ask myself, "Does this wine smell *really good*? Is the good smell *really strong*?" If the answer to both these questions is an unqualified yes, the wine scores a 4, no matter whether the pleasantness of the smell comes from its being vinous, distinct, varietal, or from bottle aging.

If the smell, on the other hand, is very, very weak, and not all that good anyway, I give the wine a zero. And if it's in between, I give it in between.

Let me interject something that applies to judging all these categories. After you've judged half a dozen bottles, trying to think about all these individual qualities of aroma and bouquet, as well as clarity, color, and all the rest, you'll find that the whole thing gets easier. Practice, even if it doesn't make perfect, will at least make you comfortable, confident, and if you keep at it, quite competent.

Acescence: 2 points

You're not through sniffing the wine, however, because you still have 2 points to award—or withhold—with your nose. These points are for the presence or absence of vinegar. In fancier language, you are testing for acescence, or volatile acid. So, take a sniff of the wine in your glass, and if you don't smell any vinegar, give the wine 2 points. If you smell vinegar very, very faintly, just the barest, tiniest whiff, give the wine 1 point. And if the vinegar smell is strong, give it zero. So much for acescence.

Now we're going to do what you wanted to do all along, namely, taste the wine.

The question of how to taste a wine has been discussed exhaustively in any number of learned books. In this book, however, neither you nor I is going to become exhausted by the subject.

If, as a result of your experimentation with wine, you want to delve into which area of the tongue contains the taste buds that detect and measure the presence of sugar, and other interesting technicalities, you will find the subject a rewarding one. But it won't make an enormous difference in your ability to judge wine.

Developing your own tasting procedure

Each person has to determine just what constitutes his or her most productive tasting procedure once the wine gets into the mouth. Some people chew it, some people inhale through the mouth, thus aerating the wine (and occasionally getting a dollop down the windpipe), some press the tongue against the roof of the mouth and raise their eyebrows expectantly. Some purse their lips and suck in their cheeks as though they had just bitten into a green persimmon. Some gargle.

I recommend them all. That is, I recommend that you experiment with your wine and your tongue and the roof and sides of your mouth, and a little bit of air and a little bit of solemnity, and see what happens. Because, only by experimentation, trial and error, the pragmatic approach, can you determine whether there is, or is not, a preferred system of tasting for you.

Myself, I run the wine around in my mouth with my tongue, hold it, breathe through my nose, and think. I try very hard to remember other wines I have tasted, and I try to think just what words best describe whatever it is that is going on inside my mouth and nose. It's not a ritual. It's simply an attempt to let my senses do the job they're supposed to do, namely to identify and catalog those sensations that please them most.

To spit or not to spit

When a professional wine taster has evaluated his mouthful of wine, what does he do? Correct! He spits it out.

We won't do that.

Recently I read a book on wine that outlined the procedure for giving a sit-down wine-tasting party. The author recommended "spitting buckets . . . one for every two guests."

Forget your bucket, gentle reader. You are the bucket. That's half the fun of tasting wine.

True, your ability to discriminate subtle differences between wines diminishes as you drink more of them, but it also diminishes, though not so rapidly, as you taste more and more wines and spit them out. There is a fatigue factor in both tasting and smelling, and it's pretty hard to avoid. So, unless you are tasting a dozen or more wines in a side-by-side tasting, or judging wines for the Los Angeles County Fair, you can forget about spitting them out.

That doesn't mean that you can gulp your wine, however. Take a middle road. Take enough wine into your mouth to get a good, honest taste, evaluate it, think about it, put your evaluation into words, and then swallow.

Acidity: 2 points

In our battery of taste tests, the first thing we try to evaluate is called "total acid." This is a test of whether the wine feels refreshing to your mouth, or flat, or soapy, or sharp.

Your wine, as you might suspect, shouldn't be

too sharp or too flat. Too much acid content makes it sharp, too little makes it flat. To be pleasant, the wine should hit somewhere in the middle ranges, making your mouth feel refreshed. A wine may have a fairly high acidity and still be considered good, provided it is well balanced. It will taste agreeably fresh, and the words that will spring to your mind as you hold it in your mouth are these: "pleasantly tart."

At first, total acid is a tough category to which to assign your zero, 1 point, or 2 points, chiefly because you have probably never tried to assess a wine that way before. But after you've tried a few bottles with that particular characteristic in mind, concentrating for a moment or two solely on that single aspect, you should begin to be able to mark your scorecard with aplomb, and get on to the next category.

 Sugar: 1 point

The next category is sugar. It's worth 1 point.

Actually, sugar and acid have to balance one another. If a wine is too sweet, you won't want to serve it with a meal, except perhaps with the dessert. And if it's totally devoid of sugar content, the acidity may come through in a rather unpleasant fashion.

So, how sweet is just sweet enough to win the 1 point we have to offer for the sugar category? What I do is ask myself whether the sweetness is so pronounced that it's the first thing I notice about the wine. If so, I will probably score a zero for sugar. Similarly, if the sugar content is so low that I'm left only with a sensation of acidity, I again give it a zero. Everything in between scores 1 point.

Body: 1 point

Body, the next category, is easier to score. Like sugar, it's only worth 1 point. You should award that point to your wine if it is pleasantly full and viscous, or put another way, if it is not thin and watery. Body is something you feel in your mouth, not something you taste. It's the texture of the wine, and if your wine doesn't have any texture, give it a zero.

There's another way you can judge body, and that's by swirling the wine in the glass to make it climb the sides. When you stop swirling, watch the wine slide down the side of the glass. If it leaves a thick transparent film that is slow to rejoin the rest of the wine, and if there are a large number of fat, slow-moving "legs" moving down the sides of the glass, you have another indication that the wine has good body. If the wine is watery, the film will break up into streaks rather quickly. Incidentally, you should expect red wines to have considerably more body than whites.

Flavor: 2 points

We come now to flavor, a 2-point category. This should be a very complex and difficult category, but it isn't. Because, in the final analysis, it simply consists of answering the question "Does it taste good?"

"Good" is pleasant, clean, fruity, rich, balanced, full, spicy, tasty, yummy, any way you want to put it. Your mouth knows what tastes good to you, so trust it. And if the wine tastes really yummy, give it 2 points. Fairly yummy, give it 1 point. Not yummy at all, zilch.

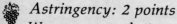 *Astringency: 2 points*

We are now closing in on the final two scoring categories. The next to last is a 2-point category called "astringency," and if your wine makes your mouth feel rough or puckery, it won't win any points. If you wish to impress your friends, you can say that the tannin content is too high.

A small amount of astringency is not too bad a thing. In fact, a moderate amount of astringency is desirable in red wines. Wines tend to have more astringency when they're young, less as the wine ages. Wines with low astringency are described as being smooth or soft; wines with a higher astringency level are described as slightly rough, and highly astringent wines are called very rough. Obviously, very rough scores zero.

General quality: 2 points

The final category is a 2-pointer which enables you to adjust for having been too generous in any one of the preceding categories, or to improve the score of a wine that you really think is a knockout. This scoring category is called "general quality," and that's precisely what it means.

Did you really like the wine? Would you like to have another glass right now? Would you like to salt a few bottles away in your garage, closet, cellar? Would you like to serve it to your friends? If the answer to any or all of these questions is yes, give the wine the 2 points for general quality. You'll also know when to give it 1 point, and when to award it the golden zero.

What your total scores mean

Your scoring is now over. You've awarded your wine up to twenty points in ten separate categories. Now all you have to do is add up the score and compare it with the University of California's standards, which go like this:

17–20 points: Wine of outstanding characteristics

13–16 points: Sound commercial wine—no outstanding merit or defect

10–12 points: Commercially acceptable wine with noticeable defect

0–9 points: Commercially unacceptable wine

How did your wine score?

Incidentally, it's a good idea to put the date and a full description of the wine on the scorecard, verbal comments as well as the numerical scores. You should also include the price and the name of the store where you bought it. And if you have a wine you aren't quite sure about after judging it, forget it for a while.

Then, later, get another bottle and put it through the 20-point ordeal again without referring to your original scorecard until you've finished. When you compare the results of the two tastings, you should have a better answer as to whether this particular wine is of sufficient quality to earn a place in your cellar.

It is possible, of course, that you may feel slightly resentful about the elaborateness of the University of California 20-point evaluation system. In fact, you may be telling yourself, "Wow, I don't want to go through that rigamarole every time I open a bottle of

		SEVEN OAKS ZINFANDEL $4.59 / GALLON SAM'S 6.22.77		LAKEVILLE ZINFANDEL $3.89 / GALLON DANTE LIQUORS 6.22.77		SANTAREEN ZINFANDEL $4.99 / GALLON SAM'S 6.22.77	
Brand Type of Wine Price Supplier Date Tasted							
Appearance	0-2	2	VERY CLEAR	1	FAINT, FAINT HAZE	2	VERY CLEAR
Color	0-2	1	A BIT ON THE LIGHT SIDE	2	RICH, RUBY RED	2	MEDIUM RED
Aroma, Bouquet	0-4	2	PLEASANT, FRUITY A BIT RELUCTANT	1	ACCEPTABLE, BUT A BIT STUFFY, DANK	2	FAINT BUT NICE CLEAN, MATURE FRUIT
Acescence	0-2	2	OKAY	2	OKAY	2	OKAY
Total Acid	0-2	1	SLIGHT SHARPNESS	1	A TRACE FLAT	2	REFRESHING, PLEASANT
Sugar	0-1	1	DRY	0	SWEETISH	1	DRY
Body	0-1	1	GOOD "LEGS"	1	GOOD	1	GOOD MOUTH-FEEL
Flavor	0-2	1	PLEASANT, BUT FAIRLY ORDINARY	0	MUSTY TASTE	1	OKAY - NOTHING SPECIAL
Astringency	0-2	1	A LITTLE ROUGH	1	SOME ROUGHNESS	2	CRISP, PLEASANT
General Quality	0-2	1	SOUND, AVERAGE	0	BELOW AVERAGE	1	SLIGHTLY ABOVE AVERAGE, OKAY
TOTAL	0-20	13	PERFECTLY OKAY BUT NOT FOR PARTIES	9	DON'T BUY AGAIN	16	BETTER THAN AVERAGE. AN ENJOYABLE WINE AND A GOOD BUY.

wine!" If this is the case (and it is with me), you may wish to move on to a somewhat simpler system that may, in the long run, do the job just as well.

The value of the U.C. system, of course, is that it makes you think about a great many individual wine characteristics, one at a time. This is something that most people have never done, and I am highly in favor of everyone who is interested in wine learning and practicing the U.C. system until he or she feels comfortable with the idea of sorting out the complexities.

The Nelson 2-3-4-5 system

The shortcoming of the U.C. system is that it is rather cumbersome. So, in case you don't have the time or the inclination to go through each of the steps, you may wish to go with what I call the Nelson 2-3-4-5 system. It's simple and easy to remember, and if you've tried the U.C. system enough times so that you're familiar with each of the components that go to make up a good wine, you'll find that they all fit into the 2-3-4-5 system.

As a little simple addition will show you, the 2-3-4-5 system is a 14-point system. It scores like this:

Eyes	2 points
Nose	3 points
Mouth	4 points
Brain	5 points

Obviously, the eyes category covers clarity, color, and visual assessment of the wine's body. The nose is responsible for aroma and bouquet. The mouth handles body, flavor, and acidity.

That leaves the brain with five big points to give out for overall quality. My own practice is to award these points by taking a second look, a second smell, a second taste, and deciding just how well these first three categories combine to make me smack my lips and say, "By George, *that* is a good wine!"

For a sample of a marked 2-3-4-5 scorecard, see page 65.

 Your eyes, your nose, your mouth, your brain
There are, of course, many other ways to score wines, and many kinds of scorecards. In the end, however, all the systems come down to the same thing, namely, taking evidence with your eyes, your nose, your mouth, and integrating these impressions with your brain.

At the beginning of this chapter, assuming you can remember back that far, I said that the best way to evaluate a wine is in the company of other similar wines. Naturally, if you and your luncheon companion are evaluating a restaurant bottle, you won't have a second wine standing by to serve as a standard.

If, on the other hand, you are in your own kitchen, staring at four red wines that call themselves Burgundies, and you want to figure out which, if any, you should buy more of, then you'd better resign yourself to the joyful task of opening all four bottles and testing each wine against the others.

	VIRAGO	BROOKFIELD	RIVER HILL	EL VERANO
Brand	VIRAGO	BROOKFIELD	RIVER HILL	EL VERANO
Type of Wine	BURGUNDY	BURGUNDY	BURGUNDY	BURGUNDY
Price	$4.25/GALLON	$5.19/GALLON	$2.89/GALLON	$7.10/GALLON
Supplier	LOU'S LIQUORS	LOU'S	BIG M LIQUORS	TORRANCE SUPER
Date Tasted	5·3·77	5·3·77	5·3·77	5·3·77
2	CLEAR DEEP RUBY — 2	CLEAR MEDIUM RED LOTS OF "LEGS" — 2	WATERY, LOOKS LIKE A PALE ROSÉ. CLEAR, HOWEVER — 1	DEEP, RICH RED, ALMOST PURPLE — 2
3	FAINT BUT PLEASANT. SLIGHT FLORAL OVERTONES — 1	FRUITY, PLEASANT, SIMPLE, A BIT RELUCTANT. — 1+	GODAWFUL! ACRID, CHEMICAL — 0	PLEASANT, FRUITY, WITH SPICY OVERTONES; OUTDOORSY! — 2+
4	DRY, ACIDIC, ALMOST ROUGH; TART, FRESH — 1+	A LITTLE SWEET, A LITTLE FLAT, BUT NOT BAD — 2	COTTON CANDY, THIN, FLAT, VULCANIZED — 0	LIVELY, SLIGHTLY TART, SMOOTH, PLEASANT AFTERTASTE — 3
5	SIMPLE, CLEAN TASTE. OKAY BUT NOT SPECIAL. — 3	SOUND AND PLEASANT. MIGHT BLEND WITH SOMETHING ACIDIC — 3	UNDRINKABLE, EVEN BY ME! — 0	A REAL FIND! A NICE WINE FOR COMPANY. — 4
14	7+	9	1	11+

Enlist some confederates
The best way to do it is to enlist some confederates. This means your wife, husband, paramour, alternate-life-style chum, neighbor, fellow bargain hunter, or whatever. From two to half a dozen people make a nice group. Larger than that becomes a production, except when you're giving a wine-tasting party, in which case you expect a production.

Letting red wines breathe . . .
Naturally, you want to have all four of your red wines at the same temperature. And you want to open them all at the same time. If you can, open them about thirty to forty-five minutes before you plan to taste them. Opening them early gives them time to breathe and develop the maximum amount of aroma, bouquet, and flavor. And a wine that tastes sharp on opening may smooth out after it's had a chance to come in contact with air for a while.

Anonymity is important to success
Another thing you want to do is to make sure that your fellow judges (and you yourself, if you can arrange it) never actually see the bottles, or, more important, the labels. The problem is that when any one of us sees a bottle of wine bearing a label that reads Margaux or Château Latour, we unconsciously predispose ourselves to think that the wine is going to be pretty good. And, like a self-fulfilling prophecy, the wine often has to be pretty bad before we stop thinking it's pretty good.

Naturally, there are limits to our credulity, but we want to eliminate as many variables as possible in our quasi-scientific test. So, one we will want to eliminate is any possible identification of the wine through seeing the shape of its bottle or its label.

Obviously, someone has to run the test, so someone has to know which wine is which. Unfortunately, if you want the test to run right, this person frequently turns out to be you.

Okay, let's say you've assembled a few fellow scientists, and you've opened your four bottles of red wine.

You should, if you've got enough glassware, give each taster four glasses, so he or she can have all four wines available simultaneously in order to make the side-by-side comparisons we've already talked about. It's nice if the glasses are all alike, and nicer yet, if all are more or less like the standard 8 or 10-ounce wineglass you encounter in most restaurants. If you haven't got sixteen or twenty identical glasses, however, don't worry about it. You can taste wines in tumblers or old jelly glasses, if necessary, because the chief ingredients of a tasting are the wines and the tasters, and the glasses are merely vehicles for bringing the two together.

Number bottles and glasses

Warn your guests that they should be very careful to keep their four glasses in their original order, so that the results of the tasting don't get more than normally confused. Or, to be safer yet, attach a numbered piece of masking tape to the stem of each glass. This will completely eliminate the possibility of your guests mixing up the wines. It will help you keep them straight, too, for that matter, because once you've got everyone else fitted out with four kinds of wine, you fit yourself out, and the evaluation begins.

Since you're in charge, you can conduct your evaluation procedures any way you want, either by asking your guests to rate the wines according to the University of California system, or the Nelson 2-3-4-5 system, or simply by tasting the wines and talking about them. I'm partial to the Nelson system myself, because it's easy to explain, and because it makes even the most inexperienced guest think about at least three separate aspects of each wine without my having to deliver a long and boring lecture.

Have your scorecards ready

For either system, U.C. or 2-3-4-5, each taster needs a pencil and paper to go along with his four glasses of wine. It's not a bad idea to make up scorecards in advance, so you're sure each taster is following the same procedure.

Let's assume that you've decided to use the 2-3-4-5 system, and that you've already filled the numbered glasses. If you haven't, now's the time to do it.

Naturally, it's handy to keep the bottles nearby, in case you have to refill the glasses. If you do, you should disguise them somehow — mask them with paper, wrap them in a napkin, do whatever is necessary to make sure none of your fellow adventurers knows which is which. Some tasters soak the labels off — in room temperature water, so as not to heat or chill the wine unduly — and then mark each bottle with a piece of tape and a number corresponding to the numbers on the glasses.

This is a lot of folderol, but the anonymity is important. You now start by making your visual evaluations of all four wines, and marking your scorecard. Then you let your nose evaluate each wine in terms of aroma and bouquet, and mark your scorecard for the nose category.

Finally, of course, you taste each wine in order, going back and forth as many times as you want. After you've marked your scorecard, you're ready to chew on a piece of bread or a plain cracker, to cleanse your palate and get your taste buds back into shape for your second eye-nose-mouth evaluation, and the awarding of the final five points.

Words to drink by . . .

It's an excellent idea to write down a few words about each aspect of each wine, provided you can think of the words that describe the way the wine looks or smells or tastes.

You'll find the words hard to come by at first, and you may feel a bit affected saying that the wine has "a rather astringent mouth-feel," but it's like anything else: once you do it awhile, it gets easy.

Besides, the words are usually more useful than the numbers in helping you remember just what it was you liked about the smell of a particular wine— was it that you liked its strong, fruity aroma, or did it have an unusual spicy smell, or again, did it remind you of fresh-cut clover? If you wrote it down, you'll know.

The real pleasures of tasting

After everyone has scored the four wines, two of the greatest pleasures of wine emerge. The first is talking about them, comparing your evaluations with those of your fellow tasters. The second, of course, is drinking what's left in your glass, and refilling it and drinking some more. If someone found the first wine had a dry, fruity taste, and you thought it was a little on the sweet side, there's plenty of opportunity for both of you to taste the wine again and talk about it, and see if you feel your original evaluation still holds.

At some point, of course, you'll want to bring out the bottles and identify which was which. This will probably start another round of conversation and still more tasting, and before you know it, you will have invested a lot of very pleasant time in a very genial activity.

Other methods, other thoughts . . .

There are lots of other ways to compare wines, as well as ways to compare the abilities of different wine tasters. One such procedure is called the "triangular test" and consists of presenting a taster with three glasses, two of which contain the same wine, while the third glass contains a different wine. The taster is then asked to tell which of the three glasses contains the odd sample. This is a system that is often used in choosing people for a taste panel. It's slightly complicated, since to get a good taster it's necessary to present him with five to ten different triangular tests to make sure that he is consistent in picking the right wine. This takes a lot of time, a lot of glasses, a lot of different wines, and a lot of money. I suggest you get into this kind of testing only if you decide that the life of a professional wine taster is the only life for you.

There are a number of differing schools of thought about wine tasting. Some authorities, for example, feel that your senses are at their most discriminating when you're reasonably hungry. Some feel that tasters do their best work in the morning, when most of the rest of us are busily engaged in doing something that can't be half as much fun. Yet, there is another body of opinion that says your senses are sharpest between six and twelve in the evening, and says further that women consistently surpass men in their ability to discriminate between different tastes and smells.

The opinion that counts: Yours

Fortunately, you're at liberty to form your own body of opinion. As we agreed at the outset, what really counts is how the wine tastes to you. So, no matter what your fellow tasters may say as they sit there, sipping your wine and marking your scorecards, you are the ultimate authority. Don't forget it.

4

How you
serve it:
THE OTHER HALF OF THE WINE EQUATION

Once upon a time I read the results of an experiment in which men and women were asked to evaluate four separate cups of coffee in order to decide which of the four cups was best.

The cups into which the coffee had been poured were identical, and each was sitting in front of an opened can that was half full of ground coffee. Each can was color coded, one can brown, one blue, one red, one yellow. Nobody actually said that each cup of coffee had been made from the contents of the can in front of which it stood, but the cup placements implied it strongly.

Each person, after tasting the four cups of coffee, was asked to rank the coffees 1, 2, 3, 4, in order of preference, and to list those attributes that made the taster like or dislike each cup.

When the results were tabulated, it was found that a large majority of the tasters gave first place to the coffee sitting in front of the red can. They described it as rich, full bodied, and satisfying. The coffee in front of the brown can was adjudged a trifle strong, the coffee in front of the yellow can a bit weak. The coffee in front of the blue can, said the tasters, was bitter.

As you have probably already guessed, the four cups of coffee were identical, poured from the same pot.

The researchers concluded, as they had suspected all along, that the color of the container from which the coffee was thought to have been made was a much more powerful factor in influencing the brain's decision than the actual taste.

Put another way, the tasters transferred their visual sensations into what they believed were their taste sensations. For some reason—don't ask me why—it seemed to make a lot of sense that coffee from a red can should be richer than coffee from cans of other colors. This fact has not been lost on marketers of coffee, which is why, when you walk down the coffee aisle in any supermarket, you will see a lot of cans sporting a fair amount of red.

Coffee marketers aren't the only people who worry about their packages. It is a commonplace of consumer marketing that the look of a package will influence not only a consumer's readiness to put it in the shopping cart, but the consumer's ultimate evaluation of the product itself.

Naturally, if something tastes awful, you can't make it taste wonderful simply by putting it into a wonderful package. Within certain limits, however, since the average set of taste buds walks on extremely shaky ground, you can influence the brain's response simply by altering the size, shape, color, or general graphic design of your package.

What's the message for us impoverished wine drinkers? The message is that the enjoyment of a wine is not determined solely by the wine itself. The message is that the visual clues we give our guests when we serve them wine will most assuredly influence their perceptions. The container from which we pour the wine, the glassware into which we pour it, the manner in which we serve it, all these things will, within limits, influence our guests' evaluation and enjoyment of the wines we serve them.

Amazingly enough, you will find that these same visual cues will influence your own perceptions, even those of wines with which you are already familiar. Thus, although you're dining alone, eating last night's leftovers, the wine with which you accompany your meal will taste better if you pour it from a Swedish glass carafe into an 18-ounce balloon goblet, rather than if you slop it out of a gallon jug into a jelly glass.

Please understand that I'm not asking you to adopt a set of affectations. After all, there is absolutely nothing wrong with pouring wine from a jug into a jelly glass and enjoying it. Serving and drinking wine is not a matter of right and wrong. Thus, the suggestions I am about to make are not aimed at enabling you to "fool your friends" or "put on the dog." They are simply ideas to help you maximize your own enjoyment of the many different kinds of wine that you can afford to buy and serve, and your friends' enjoyment of them, too.

The power of confidence

The first thing to remember about serving one of your wines is this: Never apologize for a wine you are about to serve. Serve it confidently, with a smile, and without too much foofaraw. If you serve it hesitantly or say something like "Gosh, I hope this wine's okay . . .," your guest will probably get an uneasy feeling which he may transfer to his evaluation and enjoyment of the wine itself.

It's the old self-fulfilling prophecy. If you think you're going to fail, you probably will. But if you think you're going to win, well, you may not win, but you stand a much greater *chance* of winning, simply because you have a positive attitude and you're not thinking failure.

Do you remember the old story about the gold rush? A mischief-maker comes into a bar in Alaska and fabricates a rumor that they've struck a rich vein of gold on the North Fork of the Whatsis River. The effect is electric. The bar buzzes with excitement and rapidly clears as the patrons rush to get their picks and gold pans. The rumormonger watches, chortling with wicked glee, until the bar is empty. Then suddenly, he bolts for the door to get his own equipment and head for the Whatsis.

"You never know," he says, "a rumor like that could have some truth to it!"

The same psychology that applies to rumors of gold strikes also applies to wines. If someone tells us,

"I want you to taste a really superb wine," or if we are offered wine from a bottle labeled Chambertin-Clos de Bèze, or if the sommelier in a fancy restaurant pours our wine from a sparkling crystal pitcher into an elegant Baccarat wineglass, we generally figure we're in for a treat.

Our expectations are part of the treat, part of the machinery that helps make the wine taste good. We transfer our visual perceptions—and the expectations these perceptions generate—into the realm of our taste sensations, without even knowing it.

Question: Would the Chambertin-Clos de Bèze have tasted as good poured out of a Mason jar into a toothpaste glass, and served timidly with the remark, "Gee, this is all we've got, I hope it's okay . . ."?

The answer is no. But it still wouldn't have tasted bad!

 Packaging the wine experience
I have picked up many ideas about serving wine from restaurants. For example, when you order the house wine at the Fior d'Italia in San Francisco, assuming you order more than a single glass, your waiter will bring it to you in a simple, green, fifth-size bottle. The bottle will already be open; in fact, without your knowing it, it has just been filled from a gallon jug behind the bar. Nevertheless, it has a plain, decent, authentic look to it, honorable yet without pretense, and even though you have not gone through the ceremony of the cork and the tasting, there is considerable satisfaction in seeing your wine poured from this simple, unlabeled green bottle into the waiting, stemmed glass.

There is another advantage to this procedure at the Fior. You're charged only for what you pour out of the bottle.

Order the house wine at Le Bistro in New York, and your waiter will bring it in a handsome glass pitcher with straight sides and no ornamentation. The glass into which he will pour your wine will also be plain and traditional, and the whole experience will be extremely pleasant.

There are many, many kinds of pitchers suitable for serving wine, and one of the important things to remember is that there are no rules on the subject. This was brought home to me several years ago when I was charged with setting up an informal luncheon in San Francisco for fifteen visiting Frenchmen and an equal number of Americans. I selected a small Neapolitan restaurant called Tommaso's, and since I had to operate within a budget, I suggested that we have the house wine rather than something more expensive.

Lino Costa, who was in charge, immediately produced several flowered pottery pitchers, and announced that he would use them to serve the wine. Because I had never before seen wine served from flowered pottery pitchers, I suffered about five seconds of doubt. Then, as the sixth second ticked by, I realized that they were not only suitable, they were an absolutely perfect complement to the country informality of the meal, the restaurant, and the occasion.

The luncheon was a huge success, and the moral of the story is obvious: When you serve wine, you make your own rules.

At home, my wife and I serve wine from many different containers. Sometimes it's a plain green wine bottle. Sometimes the plain green wine bottle wears a handwritten label noting what kind of wine it is, when it was rebottled from a larger container into fifths, and occasionally the wine's rating on the 2-3-4-5 scale.

Sometimes we use our Italian *litros*, the common garden variety of wine carafe in which house wines are often served in restaurants. They're made of heavy glass and feature a circular glass blob on the front with a piece of lead sealed into it. They also have a line scribed near the top of the neck, showing exactly how full the jar should be in order to contain exactly one liter.

We have two of them, a green one we use for white wines, and a clear one for reds.

We also use a flowered pottery pitcher, not quite like the ones at Tommaso's, a couple of smallish cut-crystal pitchers that look very handsome when filled with red wine, one Danish decanter, very modern, and one beaker that looks as though it would be more at home in a chemistry lab than on a dinner table. It would be, in fact, because that's where it came from, and I guess that's why I like it.

We also have one large, green, unlabeled glass bottle, magnum size, and one large clear one that I bought filled with bargain Frascati, and which looks great on the table, filled with either red or white. And we have several wicker-enclosed bottles in sizes varying from a fifth to a half-gallon. I occasionally fill them and put them on the table when the menu includes spaghetti, lasagna, or some equally suitable dish. I also take them on picnics.

None of these serving containers cost me very much, but that isn't the principal reason I like them. I like them because they have a modest amount of style and charm without any particular affectation, and because they somehow make our rebottled reds and whites taste a little better than they ought to.

Take a look around your own house or apartment. Chances are you already have some pitchers or other containers that you never thought about using to serve wine, but which will do the job very nicely.

Great, cheap glasses for great, cheap wine

You can also add a little extra fillip to the occasion by the way you use your containers. For example, you might want to put two unlabeled fifths on your table, one red, one white, so your guests can have their choice. Or, if you're having more than one course, you might want to give each guest two glasses, and serve the white wine with the first course and the red with the second. Or, if you really want to freak everyone out, you can give each guest three glasses, one for the white, one for the red, and one for the sweet, slightly charged dessert wine you serve with the cherries jubilee.

This latter effort will require quite a bit of glassware, so this is probably the right time to pass along a purchasing tip. This is simply that when you are looking for glassware, you might try your local restaurant supply house. Restaurants go in and out of business with fair regularity, which means that all kinds of wineglasses move in and out of the supplier stores with the change of the tide. To find these stores, look under "Restaurant Supplies" in the yellow pages.

When you visit this kind of store, look for simple,

classic glasses that hold at least 10 ounces when filled to the brim. You might also take a look at the larger, 18-ounce balloon glasses. They cost a little more, but their extra size gives them an extra touch of class, in addition to which they're great for swirling and sniffing wine. Whichever glasses you pick, however, they'll be a little thicker than the fine crystal goblets the Queen drinks from, but for you that's an advantage, not a disadvantage. You can run your stemware through the dishwasher with minimum fear of breaking them, and the Queen can't.

One way or another, however, no matter how careful you are, you'll break some glasses. My advice is to buy an oversupply—they're fairly cheap—and not to worry. Besides, if you bought a standard restaurant model, you can always go back for more of the same.

As for pitchers, if you don't like those offered by the restaurant supply house, fortunately there are lots of attractive pitchers available in many different kinds of stores at relatively modest prices. So, use your own judgment, indulge your taste, preference, or prejudice, and you should be able to put your wines on the table in a way that gives them every possible chance of succeeding in their pleasant, humanitarian mission.

My own tastes run in favor of simple containers and simple glasses, and against serving wine from any kind of metal pitcher. I freely admit that this last is my own irrational prejudice, amply proved by the fact that I used to enjoy a particular kind of Beaujolais that came in a pull-top can. I would probably still enjoy it if it had been successful enough to survive in the U.S. market, although now that I've learned to buy in bulk and rebottle, I probably couldn't afford it any more.

Wine on picnics

While we're talking about serving wine, we should not overlook the fact that not all wine is consumed at luncheon or the dinner table. Wine is also consumed on picnics at the beach, during romantic trysts in the woods, aboard motorboats and sailboats, and just about any place that people sit down to enjoy an informal meal. One of nature's most beautiful sights, in fact, is a pair of naked green bottles lying on their sides in the shallow edge of a mountain stream, letting the icy waters cool the fragrant white wines inside.

Some purists, in fact, maintain that wine on a picnic should be drunk from the same stemmed glassware used at the dinner table. I have to admit that it makes for a pretty classy picnic, and not only the wine, but the fried chicken or peanut-butter sandwiches take on a gourmet dimension you didn't know they had. Getting the glasses back and forth without breaking them is a bit of a chore, and if you let them clank around in the trunk of your car it may be more than you can put up with. Still, if you've never sat idly beside a mountain stream, sipping cold Chablis out of a classic wineglass, maybe you ought to try it at least once.

Take a bota *to lunch*

Of course, there are lots of ways to take wine on a picnic. Take, for example, the *bota*.

I came into contact with my first working *bota* just outside an amusement park in San Sebastián, in the Basque area of Spain. A *bota*, to keep you in suspense no longer, is one of those leather flasks, nowadays usually lined with plastic, slung on a shoulder cord and intended for carrying wine wherever you want to take it.

Emptying wine from a *bota* is only slightly harder than filling one. You remove the cap, hoist the *bota* to a position slightly higher than your head, point the nozzle in the general direction of your mouth, and squeeze.

With practice, you become skilled. You hit your shirt only one time in four, and finally not at all. And, most amazing of all, the whole idea of drinking wine from a *bota* will gradually stop being a parlor trick and become a very sensible way to take wine to places where wine has never gone before.

The *bota*, you see, has licked the problem of air attacking the remaining wine in a partially emptied container. The *bota*, being flexible, collapses as the wine supply diminishes, with the result that there is no more air in the *bota* when you've drunk half the wine than there was when the *bota* was full.

Like a wine bottle, a *bota* can be immersed in a stream to cool it. Even better than a wine bottle, however, the *bota* continues to cool the wine after it has been withdrawn from the stream, thanks to the gradual evaporation of the water that has soaked into its leather cover.

Another nice thing about a *bota* is that you can forget your stemmed glassware, you can forget styrofoam cups or tin cups or plastic-coated paper cups.

The *bota* is the serving container, and each person becomes his own drinking utensil. Is it hygienic? You bet! Any number can drink from (or be bathed by) the same *bota* and still preserve the strictest standards of hygiene, since mouths and lips never touch the *bota* itself.

Botas come in many sizes, from tourist-souvenir-tiny to authentic-Spanish-large. I recommend the latter highly to anyone who likes hiking, cycling, picnicking, and the concomitant pleasures of dining al fresco with wine.

Have dinner with a porrón
The *porrón* is the indoor equivalent of the *bota*. My wife and I saw our first *porrón* in action in an elegant restaurant in Barcelona called Los Tres Gatos. A *porrón* is a large glass container shaped like a badly squashed ball. A conical glass spout protrudes from one side of the *porrón*, and a slightly flared tube rises out of the top, serving not only as a means of filling the *porrón*, but also as a handle for picking it up.

I had to marvel at the unerring accuracy and complete insouciance with which each person at a table near ours directed the stream of red wine through a long, looping arc into a slightly opened mouth. My own mouth would have been gaping as though the dentist were repairing a nether inlay.

I have seen *porróns* on sale in the United States, but only very small toylike ones, and as a result I don't have one.

If you're really adventurous, you can score a lot of points in the gee-whiz-look-at-him category by storing your wine in a wineskin. In the average American city, however, a wineskin may be a hard item to come by.

 About wineskins

I have seen only one set of authentic wineskins in my life, and that was in a restaurant in Madrid called Mesón de San Javiar, which stores its house wines in several large bullskins. A bullskin is a large skin with the bull removed and the skin sewn back together so that it is watertight, or as it turns out, winetight, and then filled with wine.

At the San Javiar, the skins rest on a big table, and when you order the house wine, the waiter takes a pitcher over to one of them, opens a spigot that has been inserted into a foreleg, and fills the pitcher. He then returns to the table and pours, and you sit for a long time staring at your filled glass, wondering whether or not to drink the wine. In the end, of course, you do, and it tastes just fine.

Like the *bota*, the wineskin solves the problem of keeping air from attacking the wine remaining in a partially emptied container. The wineskin simply collapses as the wine pours out, leaving the wine as safe from air damage as it was when the skin was full.

Neither you nor I will probably ever serve our wine from a wineskin. For us, the wineskin will simply serve to symbolize the fact that with a little investigation, thought, and experimentation, you can devise your own serving techniques to heighten your enjoyment of the wine experience.

What the wine-serving equation boils down to is

this: If there was once a right way and a wrong way to serve wine, there isn't any more. Now there are only interesting ways and unimaginative ways, and you don't have to stand on your head or pour wine from a hiking boot to make the way you serve wine interesting.

The simple ways of serving wine have plenty of charm, and the principal thing to do is to make sure you give the serving process all the care and thought it deserves. If you do, those good, sound, $2.99-or-less wines that you have selected so carefully will add a measure of enjoyment to your meal far out of proportion to their cost.

5

Great cheap wine miscellany

OR EVERYTHING THAT DIDN'T FIT INTO
ANOTHER CHAPTER

I am now going to serve you a mismatched potpourri of wine information that somehow just didn't seem to fit anywhere else.

You don't have to read it if you don't want to. If you reached this page without skipping, you have already acquired the basic tools for finding, judging, and serving great cheap wines. So, if you're in a hurry, you can omit this chapter and jump ahead to page 106 and start reading my listings of cheap wines, great and otherwise, together with my evaluations and comments.

On the other hand, if you have a few more minutes, you might as well hang around while I divest myself of a few more thoughts about wine that may or may not fit into your own ways of acquiring and appreciating wine.

Blending your own wines

The first thought I would like to offer to those splendid individuals who have kept on reading is the idea of blending your own wines. Let's say you have bought a gallon of wine that tastes pretty good, that has a clear, ruby color, good body, and a pleasing aroma, but lacks a feeling of freshness. It's just a bit too flat, a bit innocuous, a bit lacking in the tartness that would make it seem well balanced enough to score the extra points necessary to put it in your Winner's Circle.

Well, take a look at your past wine-scoring records and see if somewhere you haven't come across a wine that seemed sound, smelled and tasted good, but lost points because it was too sharp, too rough, too tingling when you swished it around your mouth and swallowed it. If you're like me and hate to pour a bottle down the sink unless it's totally undrinkable, you probably have a few fifths of such a wine hanging around the house. Maybe you bought a gallon of such a wine, used one fifth for tasting, and rebottled the other four, simply because even cheap wine costs money, and you figured the time might come when you'd be glad you had it around.

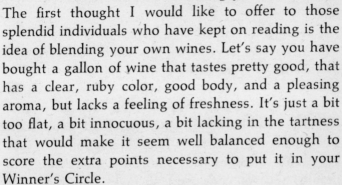

Tart helps flat, flat helps tart

Well, now is that time. Open a bottle of the flat wine and a bottle of the tart wine, and do a little experimental blending. Take three glasses, number them, and into the first glass pour one jigger of the flat wine and three jiggers of the tart one. Into the second glass pour two jiggers of each. Into the third glass, pour three jiggers of the flat wine and one jigger of the tart one.

Now you're ready to evaluate three totally new wines. You've never tasted any of them before, and neither has anyone else. You set about your task in exactly the same manner as though they were three new wines you had just brought back from your friendly neighborhood wine merchant. You score each of them on the basis of an evaluation with your eyes, an evaluation with your nose, then with your mouth, and you conclude your investigation by integrating all this sensory data in the convolutions of your brain.

Many results are possible. One of them, unfortunately, is that none of the blends will taste worth a damn. However, it is highly unlikely that the blending of these two wines will turn out to taste less good than either one of the two wines tastes separately. And it may happen that you'll stumble onto a combination that's better than either of the wines drunk all by itself.

That's what you hope happens anyway, and it's really not a far-fetched idea. After all, that's what the winemakers do. A Cabernet Sauvignon made in California, for example, only needs to contain 51 percent Cabernet grapes in order to be labeled "Cabernet Sauvignon" (unless the label states specifically, as some labels do, that the wine is made 100 percent from grapes of the Cabernet variety). As a result, most winemakers who offer a Cabernet Sauvignon do a little blending, mixing the pure Cabernet with wines from different (and usually cheaper) grapes, and tasting the results until they find the blends they want.

It takes care to grow good grapes, skill and experience to press and ferment them, and a talented palate to blend them into an interesting, well-balanced wine. Fortunately, you as a wine fancier don't have to grow the grapes or make the wine, and just as fortunately, you now have the talent and the judging criteria for deciding which wines look, smell, and taste good to you. So try some blending. Blend some reds together. Blend some whites. Blend a red with a white and make your own rosé. If you think a particular wine needs a little more flavor, try adding a fractional amount of sherry or port or whatever strikes your fancy. It's a lot of fun, and the wines you will then be able to put on your table will not be available on any other dinner table in the world!

I said you don't have to grow the grapes or make the wine, but many people do just that—particularly the latter. I recently ran into a friend on an airplane and found that he and three friends had bought 16 acres of Zinfandel grapes in Sonoma County, California. They bought it half as an investment, half as a lark, and it was rich in both. They were not only selling grapes to local vintners, but were holding back enough so that each of the four families was able to make 200 gallons each year! That's a lot of Zinfandel!

It's quite possible you may not be situated geographically or economically to repeat my friend's adventure. If you were, we might never have met in the pages of *The Poorperson's Guide to Great Cheap Wines*. Poverty, nevertheless, need not keep either of us from making our own wines if that's what we feel like doing, because it is not an expensive process.

Making your own wine

Do not fear, gentle reader, that I am now going to take you step by step through the process of making your own wine. All I am going to do is suggest that, if the idea of making your own wine intrigues you, you will probably find that it's a lot easier and a lot less expensive than you ever dreamed. You don't have to live in California or the vineyard area of New York State in order to get the ingredients, the equipment, and the know-how you need to embark on your project.

 Don't forget the Feds

But first, a word from your friendly neighborhood attorney: To make wine at home you need a permit from the Feds. It's called Treasury Form 1541, and it is simply a declaration of your intention to make some wine for in-home consumption. The form is free, and it allows the "head of household" to make up to 200 gallons a year for his or her own consumption, without paying any tax. Consult your local Internal Revenue Service office to find out where winemakers in your area get the necessary forms.

 Wine kits

The easiest way to start making wine at home is with a kit. You've probably seen them for sale in drug, liquor, or department stores. They come in a variety of sizes, suitable for making anything from a gallon on up. Ordinarily they have fairly detailed instructions on what to do, when and where to do it, and for how long. Chances are, if you follow the directions, you will find that you have made some very agreeable wines at prices that range from $.50 on up to our top limit of $2.99 a fifth and even beyond, depending on how and where you bought your ingredients, and what quality you decided to indulge in.

Kit winemakers generally make their wines from extracts. Making wine from extracts obviously doesn't have quite the same degree of romance as trampling the vintage with your own bare feet. Nevertheless, there are some very good extracts available from a variety of sources, some of which you'll find at the back of the book. Depending on the care you take and the amount of expertise you develop, they will produce some very fine, very interesting, and sometimes very unusual wines.

Besides, if you live in an apartment in New York City, you may find that one of those small-print clauses in your lease specifically prohibits, along with denial of your right to drive nails into the walls or keep a goat in your kitchen, the trampling of grapes.

Two ways to go about making wine
As in all things, there is an expensive way and a cheap way to go about making wine at home. The expensive way is to go to your wine equipment supplier and outfit yourself with a deluxe setup, everything new and shiny from the ground up. The other way is to look around your house or apartment and see how many crocks or other large stainless steel or unchipped enamelware containers you may have, in order not to have to buy any big barrels or carboys.

Also, in time, you will find plenty of use for those big gallon jugs from which you have rebottled those many fifths of wine.

You'll also need some corks, some rubber stoppers which you will fit with short lengths of glass tubing, some plastic tubing, some cheesecloth, and lots and lots of bottles for the finished product.

Naturally, you have to know what to do with all this stuff. Well, there are lots of good books on making wine, and some of them are listed in the back of this book. They range from the famous University of California Professor Maynard Amerine's *Technology of Winemaking* to Wine and the People's *Country Wine Recipes*. Basically, they're all concerned with the same process, but of course each winemaker-writer has a few tricks that are his or her own special technique for achieving perfection. As you get deeper into making your own wine, you'll undoubtedly develop tricks of your own.

Polynesian Barsac?

Making your own wine opens up all kinds of new horizons as far as your nose and mouth are concerned, because the people who supply winemaking extracts seem to try to outdo each other in coming up with new and exotic formulas. Recently, for example, I received a notice from a West Coast mail-order supplier, offering extracts that will enable home winemakers to make "June Mead, a strawberry and honey combination, sure to please on a summer evening or for a casual party . . . California Gamay, a new twist on an old favorite . . . Polynesian Barsac, a white wine that even your most knowledgeable wine snob friends won't be able to identify . . . and Date Madeira, one of our latest discoveries, great for sipping in front of the fire."

With homemade Polynesian Barsac on your table, poured from your cut-glass pitcher into your balloon goblets, how can you lose?

A last resort: Real grapes

Even though extracts represent the easiest way to make wine in your home, you shouldn't rule out the plain, old-fashioned way of making wine from real, honest-to-God grapes. Obviously, where you live has something to do with the availability of grapes in quantity. But even if you live far, far away from the vineyards of California or New York, you can still take a crack at buying grapes in quantity at your local wholesale produce market, providing you get up early enough to get there when your town's grocery-store operators are buying their daily supplies of fruit and vegetables, including grapes. It doesn't always work out, but it has been my general experience that most wholesalers don't mind selling in quantity to ordinary mortals, provided the mortals behave in a confident manner, as though they were accustomed to buying in the wholesale market every day, and pay cash.

Wine drinks

Now that you know all about how to make wine, let's move on to another subject: recipes for wine drinks. There are at least a thousand of them, but in an

Olympian effort to simplify, let me state my gross generalization that they are all variations of two great basic concoctions, sangría and hot mulled wine.

Sangría, as you undoubtedly already know, is a Spanish mixture, usually consisting of red wine, citrus juice, and sugar in varying quantities, and always drunk cold. Mulled wine, on the other hand, is generally a mixture of wine, sugar, and spice-cupboard miscellany, and is always drunk hot.

Sangría: The classic recipe

Let me start you off with what I consider to be the classic recipe for sangría. Let me also state at the outset that there are at least 99 recipes for sangría, all of which are claimed as classic recipes by the people to whom they are near and dear. I found this out in Spain one long, hot summer by ordering a lot of sangría, and by doing a lot of watching, question-asking, and many gallons worth of tasting. It was an arduous task, but when you love your work, you're willing to make certain sacrifices.

The classic recipe, therefore, is simply the recipe I liked best, and here is how you make it. Take two oranges, one lemon, one fifth of good red wine, a bottle of brandy (no, you won't use the whole bottle!), and the family sugar bowl (you won't use all the sugar, either).

Juice the oranges and the lemon. Before you do, however, cut a nice round slice out of the middle of the lemon and one out of the oranges. You'll float these on top of the pitcher of sangría when it's all finished. Pour the lemon and orange juice into a glass or pottery pitcher, add about three heaping table-spoons of sugar and some brandy ("some" is up to you; I generally put in 3 to 6 ounces), and stir the mixture up with a long-handled wooden spoon. Final-ly, pour the fifth of wine in, and stir some more.

Now taste your concoction. Chances are it may need a little more sugar, but that will depend on whether you like it a little on the sweet side, as I do. When tasting, it's not a bad idea to pour a little bit of your sangría over some ice and taste it after it has cooled, because that's the way you're going to drink it, and it may taste slightly different when cold.

When you have your sangría at the desired degree of sweetness, float the orange and lemon slices on top of the mixture, and you're ready to serve. Take several tall glasses, put three of four or five ice cubes into each one, give the sangría a final stir with the wooden spoon, and fill the glasses.

I presume you will know what to do next.

Sangría is an informal drink, but even informality can be elegant. So, if you managed to make a great buy on those 18-ounce balloon goblets from the restaurant supply store, trot them out right away. The sangría will look wonderful in them, and they'll make a mighty good thing taste even better.

In time, the wooden spoon with which you stir your sangría will acquire a reddish-purplish color from having sat in the pitcher, waiting to give the mixture a stir before you serve the next round. Somehow, when you open the kitchen drawer on a cold, wintry day and see this stained implement lying there, reminding you of all the good sangrías you made the summer before, it will give you a psychological lift. Mine does, anyway.

Now for the variations on the classic recipe. They are as numerous as religious sects, and each has its disciples. The first area of potential variation has to do with the fruit. Some people feel that a sangría is not a sangría unless it has a lime in it. You can substitute it for a lemon, or you can use a lime in addition to the lemon, or, if your taste buds march to a different drummer, you can make your sangría with nothing but limes, and forget the oranges and lemons.

Or you can slip in a grapefruit. Or some tangerines or tangelos or mandarin oranges. Or strawberries or raspberries or blueberries or ollalieberries. You can try making it with pineapple juice and call it Hawaiian Sangría. Or you can use peach nectar or crushed cherries or cranberry juice. You'll be putting a lot of distance between your sangría and the sangrías of Spain, but who cares? They're your taste buds—use them! I have been served sangrías with fruit cocktail floating in them, and a spoon to fish it out and eat it with. It was awfully good, and I made a mental note to try it at home sometime.

The next area of variation, and one the Spanish monkey around with quite a bit, has to do with the brandy. For example, you can omit it entirely and still have a wonderful sangría. Or you can make it with gin instead. (That's the way they made it for me once in Toledo—the one near Madrid, not the other one.) Or you can add a combination of brandy and gin, or rum, light or dark, or a touch of fruit-flavored liqueur or a trace of crème de menthe or orange curaçoa, or whatever you happen to have in your liquor cabinet that seems as though it might fit.

Concentration vs. dilution

Since the objective of a sangría is to refresh you, not to make you drunk, you don't want to add so much liquor that you turn the concoction into a bomb. The addition of a hard liquor is for flavor and character, and it's up to you to decide just how much flavor and character your particular sangría needs. Some people, in fact, like to go in the other direction and make the solution more dilute by adding ginger ale, a lemon-lime or other fruit-flavored soft drink, or plain old club soda. Experimentation is the order of the day.

White-wine sangría

Speaking of noble experiments, last summer the Nelson Laboratory of Sangría Research came up with a white-wine sangría, a notable invention that I now offer to a waiting world. You make it in exactly the same way as red-wine sangría, except that you use any one of your inexpensive white wines instead of one of your inexpensive reds. I served mine in our balloon glasses on one of the hottest afternoons of the summer, and there are now rumors floating around that I may be a candidate for a Nobel Prize.

As far as I know the Nobel Prize for Sangría made with Rosé Wine has yet to be considered. So there's still time for *you* to make *your* mark in this world.

Now, about hot mulled wine. Hot mulled wine

goes with skiing, sledding, rainy days in November or March, and that terrible feeling you have in your throat just before you get a cold. In other words, it is a refresher when your hands and toes are cold, and an effective medication to boot.

Hot mulled wine: the classic recipe

So here's the classic recipe for hot mulled wine. Like all other classic recipes, every hot mulled winemaker has his or her own formula, which to his or her own taste is the only real classic recipe.

Mine starts with cloves, nutmeg, and cinnamon, all of which have to be ground up pretty well before you can begin. I use about a teaspoon of cloves, a single cinnamon stick two or three inches long, and a small amount of whole nutmeg—about one-eighth of one, if you're good at subdividing nutmegs.

Grind them up any way you want, but grind them well. You can grate the cinnamon stick on a kitchen grater as a starter, and then put the smallish pieces into a nutmeg grinder along with the cloves and the nutmeg. If you haven't got a nutmeg grinder, try a pepper grinder, and if you haven't got a pepper grinder, try a mortar and pestle. If you haven't got a mortar and pestle or a pepper grinder or a nutmeg grinder, you're in deep trouble.

Okay, you have now ground up the cloves, nutmeg, and cinnamon, one way or another. Put these spices into the top of a double boiler along with half a cup of sugar, three tablespoons of lemon juice, a fifth of your best cheap red wine, and a cup and a half of Port wine. Heat up the mixture, stirring occasionally, until the sugar is completely dissolved and the whole thing is nice and hot. It takes about twenty minutes, more or less.

Serving hot mulled wine

Once the mixture is heated, you're on your own, except for the fact that I never like to let you go off on your own without a word or two about serving. Hot mulled wine is frequently served in pottery mugs, because they help keep it hot, or in little glass cups, because that's what your local liquor store will rent you if you don't feel you have appropriate vessels for your guests to drink their hot mulled wine out of.

Like everything else, however, you can drink hot mulled wine out of a lot of different containers. Mugs are nice; little glass cups with handles are nice; but wine glasses can be nice, too, especially the smaller sizes. The big sizes let the hot wine cool off too fast. The smaller size, however—say, the 10-ounce—holds a suitable amount of hot mulled wine, and the stem lets you hold the concoction without getting second-degree burns.

It's nice to float a lemon round on top of each serving. True, it tends to get in the way when you drink it, but it adds a touch of style that your guests will just have to learn to put up with.

Variations on a theme

Hot mulled wine, how do I alter thee? Let me count the ways. If this were a recipe book, I would fill it with formulae for Fish House Punch, Wine Syllabubs, and other exotic hot wine drinks. Since it is not a recipe book, I will simply direct you to cookbooks, other wine books, books for the home bartender, and the like, where you will find a bewildering array of recipes for hot mulled wine, not to mention wine punches, and where you are sure to find at least one mixture whose name, or ingredients, or general horsepower appeals to you.

In order not to put you completely at the mercy of other books, however, I will simply state that, in general, adulteration of the classic hot mulled wine recipe begins in the area of the spices used. There is ample precedent for fooling around with mixtures that contain allspice, mint, peppermint, bay leaves, sweet basil, dill, cardamon, paprika, and you-name-it.

The next step in fooling-around-with-hot-mulled-wine gets into the kinds and amounts of fruit you use. My classic recipe calls for lemon juice, but you can't go wrong with the addition of orange juice, lime juice, grape juice, cherry juice, cranberry juice, pineapple juice, and so on.

The final adaptation, naturally, has to do with the basic ingredient of hot mulled wine, namely the wine itself. My classic recipe calls for some red wine and some Port. Instead of the red wine, however, you might try some white wine, especially if you stay toward the citrus side of things in the rest of your mixture. Hot white-wine punch is as rare as white-wine sangría, and you'll never know how good it is until you try it.

 The frontiers of science
Instead of adding Port to the classic recipe, you can try adding Sherry instead, or Muscatel or Tokay, or even a bit of rum or brandy. Or you can try mixtures. The

true scholar and scientist, which is what you must be to have read this far, is never satisfied with stock answers. The true scientist presses on to the very limits of knowledge, questioning, experimenting, adding champagne or ginger ale or whatever strikes his fancy, and then submitting to his or her taste buds the responsibility for answering the awesome question: Does it really taste good, or did I blow it completely?

Instant champagne: The light that failed

So much for hot and cold running wine. Let me tell you about my brilliant concept for making champagne in a seltzer bottle.

I bought my seltzer bottle in a secondhand store in San Anselmo, California, and my CO_2 cartridges from the liquor store. I then washed my new toy, filled it with white wine, inserted a CO_2 cartridge, and put it in the fridge to cool off. Two hours later, I started filling glasses.

The result? Well, some ideas are brilliant in conception and real dogs in execution. This one was a dog. All that came out was foam. When it settled, it was flat and ordinary. The moral, therefore, dear reader, is simply that while one must be resourceful and adventuresome in one's attitude toward wine, one cannot expect to score a touchdown on every play.

The end nears

We are now approaching the end of the book. Alas, says the wordy author, who has an irresistible urge to keep on talking about wine indefinitely. Hurrah, says the faithful reader, who wants to *get on with it!*

The author's brow wrinkles. He asks himself: What have I left out? Some words of wisdom, perhaps:

🍇 *Great, cheap wine: Nothing stands still*

I counsel you not to expect anything in your personal wine equation to stay the same forever. This applies to the sources of good, cheap wines, because the sources will change. Even as I am writing this book, new wine outlets are springing up in many areas of the country, large stores that specialize in wines—cheap wines, expensive wines, wines that were once expensive and are now being "closed out" at bargain prices because they didn't sell, wines by the bottle and wines by the case. Look for these stores, they're spreading.

The same goes for rating the wines you find: Don't expect the evaluations you make this year to hold up forever. For one thing, the wines themselves will change. Even the vintners who try to maintain a constant product year after year find that they can't always do it. And the small winery whose wine you consider outstanding this year may be gobbled up next year by a giant company more attracted by the equity in the label than the red stuff in the bottle. This, too, can change the product.

What's more, your own taste preferences may change. This is a common and very normal circumstance, and you shouldn't let it bother you. All it means is that your appreciation of smells and tastes, like your appreciation of music or art or literature or sports or fashions, is bound to change over time. So don't worry if one day you find that one of your favorite red wines doesn't hold the same charm for you that it once did. Maybe your tastes are maturing. So don't chalk it against the wine. Chalk it in favor of your educated taste buds, and set out to find yourself some new wines to enjoy.

The agony and the ecstasy

In the end, you'll find that nothing in the wine equation ever really stands still. Not the finding, not the evaluating, not even the serving. That's part of what makes the pursuit of good, affordable wines so enjoyable. Every gallon, every fifth, every glass can be a richly anticipated experience, either a new and pleasant meeting with an old friend, or an introduction to a mysterious stranger who must be sized up, and who may, in time, become another valued member of your inner circle.

But now the time has come for you to get started. Are your eyes sharp, your nose clear, your taste buds quivering in nervous anticipation? They are?

Good! Go to it! And good luck!

PART TWO

The Wine Index

AND ALL THAT

6

Disclaimers, excuses, and more disclaimers

What follows is a list of 418 wines I have bought, tasted, evaluated, loved, hated, been fascinated by, or found boring. I picked them from a much larger list of wines I have evaluated, as being broadly representative of what's out there waiting for you.

I bought every last one of these wines off the shelf in a liquor store, just the way you do. There were no gifts from vintners or wholesalers, no "introductory bottles," no freebies.

It is my list, compiled by my eyes, my nose, my mouth, my brain. It is not your list (although you're welcome to it), because you may hate the wine I loved and love the wine I hated.

Remember: Wines can change
I have rated each of these wines on the basis of my 14-point eye-ear-nose-brain system. If your evalua-

tion turns out different from mine, don't immediately assume our tastes are different. Instead, remember, as I pointed out in the closing paragraphs of the last chapter, wines do change. They can change from year to year, from shipment to shipment, from bottle to bottle in the same case. It is possible that if I were sitting in your kitchen, taste-testing with you, evaluating a wine I had previously given a high score, I might at this later time find it just as deficient as you do. (On the other hand, let's hope we'd both find it terrific!)

Symbols to help you find your way
To help you find the higher-rated wines easily, I have identified them with wineglass symbols, as follows:

This number of wineglasses in the Index . . .	. . . means this rating on the 14-point scale:
	14
♀♀♀♀♀	13+
	13
	12+
♀♀♀♀	12
	11+
	11
♀♀♀	10+
	10
	9+
♀♀	9
	8+
♀	8

Distribution key . . .

You'll also find that each listing has a reference to distribution, a letter—A, B, C, or X—that will give you a rough idea of whether you're likely to find the wine in your city. Here's the key:

A = Available in most major cities, and in many stores in those cities.

B = Available in many cities, but you may have to search to find a store that carries it.

C = Limited distribution, both as to number of cities and number of stores. But still worth a try.

X = Distribution so meager you'll probably never find it. A phenomenon, a freak, a miracle.

Incidentally, the letters refer to the distribution of the *brand* of wine—for example, Paul Masson—and not necessarily to that particular wine within the brand—for example, Paul Masson California Chenin Blanc. At best, wine distribution is chancy and unpredictable, so it's just not possible to pinpoint the distribution of each individual wine. Still, if you can find the brand, maybe you can persuade the storekeeper to try to get hold of the particular wine you want to try.

 The full name is important

Each wine in the Index carries its full name, and the name and location of the company that puts it on the market. It's important to keep the full name in mind, because one vintner may put out several different

Burgundies. One may be labeled "Jones Brothers California Burgundy," another at a slightly higher price "Jones Brothers North Coast Counties Burgundy," and a third at a still higher price "Jones Brothers Vintage Burgundy 1973." Chances are, only the first will fall within our $2.99-a-fifth guidelines. So take care.

"Made by" vs. "Produced by"

Each listing also states that the wine was "produced and bottled by," or "made and bottled by," or "cellared and bottled by" a particular vintner. In the case of California wines, this is a very rough guide to how much of the wine in the bottle was actually fermented and finished by the company that put it into the bottle.

If the label states "produced and bottled by," then at least 75 percent of the wine was fermented and finished by that winery. If the label says "made and bottled by," then only 10 percent of the wine need have been produced by the winery, and the other 90 percent or some portion of it may have been bought from another source and blended into the final product. If the label says anything else—"cellared," "vinted," "bottled," "perfected," or any long and glorious combination of these words, then none of the wine in the bottle need have been produced by that winery.

The fact that the label says simply "Bottled by Jones Brothers Winery" doesn't mean the wine is no good, however. It may be excellent. Its goodness will simply depend on the ability of the Jones Brothers to *buy* good wine, rather than on their ability to make it.

This may mean that Jones Brothers wines will be subject to more variation from year to year or from batch to batch, but if the Jones Brothers are smart, careful, and normally lucky, quality variation may not be a problem.

All about price . . .

Finally, some words about price. First, the prices in the Index don't include tax. Second, prices vary from city to city, from state to state, from coast to coast. California wines are generally—but not always— cheaper in California than in New York or Washington, D.C. Wines imported from Europe frequently— but not always—cost less in the East than they do in the West. And so on.

In the Index, therefore, I've shown not just a price, but a price *range* for each wine listed. This range is an amalgam of the most recent prices observed at the shelf or listed in the price-listing books in major U.S. cities at the time the Wine Index went to press. The prices won't tell you to-the-penny how much a particular wine is going to cost you, but they will let you know whether the wine you're interested in is in the $.99 or $1.99 or $2.99 price area. Actually, they'll probably give you a closer idea than that, but that's a start, anyhow.

Inflation has the last word

One more word about price. In a book like this, as in books that describe bargains in foreign travel, it's hard to make prices stand still. Inflation boosts the prices of most products almost daily. In the past couple of years, though, wine has resisted that trend. Thanks to abundant harvests in California and other parts of the world, we have been swimming in wine.

Now, however, California faces drought conditions. Shortage of rain and rationing of irrigation water have brought drastic predictions for future grape output. The results, for wine drinkers in general and for this book's Wine Index in particular, may be that prices could soon begin to climb again, in a dismal effort to outdistance those in effect as we go to press.

Should this happen, your self-help tools for finding and judging wines will be even more valuable than before. Your eyes, nose, mouth, and brain should be able to lead you to bargains in any kind of economic situation.

A word about language and wine snobbery

A next-to-last word—about language. Talking about wine can be as much of a game as "where'd-you-go-to-school-and-who-do-you-know." I've choked over hearing someone describe a wine as "a feisty, truculent little red," and, believe it or not, I've heard people say, "The bouquet reminds me of violets soaked in prune juice." Was that *wine* they were talking about?

Well, I'm sure I've made some similarly stupid comments in the Wine Index you're about to explore. If so, please remember that I've been seriously exposed to this malady for a good many years, and it would be a miracle if I didn't contract the disease now and again. Nevertheless, I've tried to avoid jargon and use the English language to give you some idea of which wines are dry, sweet, fruity, tart, and so forth, and if I get carried away from time to time in my descriptions, just draw a line through the offensive word or phrase, and read on.

Finally, let me say to you, dear reader, and to retailers, wholesalers, and to the winemakers themselves, I know I've probably omitted some brand or some type of wine that you desperately want included in this Index. Please believe me, I'm sorry. Maybe I can cover them some other time.

 Let's go!

So, now, without further qualification or disclaimer, here they are. They're listed in three categories: Reds, Whites, and Pinks. Happy tasting—I hope you have a wonderful time!

7

Red Wines

𝅘𝅥𝅮𝅘𝅥𝅮𝅘𝅥𝅮𝅘𝅥𝅮 ADRIATICA CABERNET FROM ISTRIA   Produced &
bottled by Adriatica, Istria, Yugoslavia. Rating: 11+.
Distribution: B. You'll like this brisk, zesty wine from
Yugoslavia. You'll like its rich, churchy-red color, and
you'll like its nose—fresh, intrusive, fruity, with floral
overtones. You'll like its spicy tart flavor, its vigor, its
fruit, its excellent balance. Now, go find a bottle! Price
range: 24 oz, $2.39–2.69.

AKADAMA LIGHT RED   Produced & bottled by Suntory,
Ltd., Tokyo & Osaka, Japan. Rating: 6. Distribution:
A. If you like the Italian wine known as Lambrusco,
you may like this sweet, flat, syrupy wine, provided it
has been well chilled. The color is medium red, with
orange tones. The nose and taste are clean but
cloying. I'm sure this wine has its followers, and
maybe it's an acquired taste. Price range: 25.4 oz,
$1.59–1.99.

♀ ALMADÉN CALIFORNIA BARBERA   Made & bottled by Almadén Vineyards, Los Gatos, California. Rating: 8. Distribution: A. This is a fruity, dryish wine with a moderate acid balance. The nose is assertive, decent enough, but with a sort of closed-window stuffiness that detracts. On balance, though, generally pleasing. Price range: 25.6 oz, $1.99–2.25.

♀♀♀♀ ALMADÉN CALIFORNIA BURGUNDY   Made & bottled by Almadén Vineyards, Los Gatos, California. Rating: 12+. Distribution: A. My most recent bottle of this crimson Burgundy had a lovely, ripe nose that seemed to show good breeding, perfect fruit, and a happy blending of youth and maturity. The taste was mouth-filling, velvety and rich, semidry, with a pleasing tart edge. Try it, and see what you think. Price range: 25.6 oz, $1.99–2.25.

♀♀♀ ALMADÉN CALIFORNIA GRENOIR ORIGINAL   Made & bottled by Almadén Vineyards, Los Gatos, California. Rating: 11. Distribution: A. This is an unusual wine, and you owe it to yourself to try it. It has a fresh, exhilarating bouquet, full of fruits and berries and sunshine, and in the mouth it's rich, rounded, full of fruit, and has a modest acid balance. It's a wine with character, and a good value. Try it, and see if you agree. Price range: 25.6 oz, $2.39–2.69.

♀ ALMADÉN CALIFORNIA MOUNTAIN RED BURGUNDY Made & bottled by Almadén Vineyards, Los Gatos, California. Rating: 8. Distribution: A. This crimson Burgundy has a very reserved nose. There's fruit in it, in a rather restrained way, and this same somber approach carries over into the taste. It's a bit dignified, the fruit is muted, it's refreshing, you may like it a lot, but don't expect it to be jolly. Price range: 25.6 oz, $1.79–2.10.

ALMADÉN CALIFORNIA MOUNTAIN RED CLARET   Made & bottled by Almadén Vineyards, Los Gatos, California. Rating: 7. Distribution: A. The color: medium red. The nose: tolerable, but with a whiff of wet cellar floors. The taste: sturdy, coarse, hearty, with a slight trace of bitterness. A decent wine, but just not a very refined one. Price range: 25.6 oz, $1.79–2.10.

ALMADEN CALIFORNIA ZINFANDEL   Made & bottled by Almadén Vineyards, Los Gatos, California. Rating: 7. Distribution: A. This clear, clean-looking, medium-red wine has a dank, musty nose and a slight sharpness that I found unappealing. The taste is fruity and simple, but a little too rough and astringent to go with anything but something hot and spicy. Price range: 25.6 oz, $2.39–2.69.

♀ AMIGO HERMANOS ROCAMAR   Bottled by Bodegas Amigo Hermanos, Reus, Spain. Rating: 8+. Distribution: X. This import is dark and purply and promising. The nose has pleasant spicy components that often turn up in Spanish wines. In the mouth it has a refreshing flavor, good acid, and a certain dignity. It's a nice surprise to find an interesting wine such as this at a price like this one carries. If you're an Iberia freak, this one will make you very happy. Price range: 24 oz, $1.19–1.39.

ANJOU ROUGE CEPAGE CABERNET   Produced by Robin-Thuleau, Rablay-sur-Lyon, France. Rating: 4. Distribution: C. What a label! Terrific! What a wine . . .

yeccchh! If all you want to do is to look at a gorgeous label and a handsome wine, this is the one for you. But if you like to smell, taste, and even drink wine, you'll find the aroma and taste of this one stemmy and dirty, sour, overly astringent, and barely drinkable, if drinkable at all. Price range: 24 oz, $1.19–1.39.

ARGENTINE TRUMPETER CABERNET SAUVIGNON   Elaborado y envasado por Bodegas Esmeralda, S.A., Mendoza, Argentina. Rating: 7. Distribution: B. Argentina has many fine wines. Fortunately, a number of them cost less and taste better than this nationally promoted example. The color is medium red with orange overtones. The nose has a dilute quality to it, and the taste is common, unexciting, flat, lacking in character or verve. ¡Qué lástima! Price range: 24 oz., $2.89–3.19.

♀♀ ARMAND ROUX BERGERAC RED TABLE WINE   Bottled and shipped by Maison A. Roux, France. Rating: 9+. Distribution: C. The color is a bit on the light side, clear and brilliant, and the wine shows good legs. The nose is somewhat formal and aristocratic, and while the wine's performance in the mouth will not win a world championship, it is still extremely pleasant, perhaps lacking the complexity promised by the handsome label, but still a very enjoyable wine. Price range: 24 oz, $1.49–1.99.

♀ B & G COSTIÈRES DU GARD   Bottled by Barton & Guestier, Blanquefort, Gironde, France. Rating: 8. Distribution: A. There's not a whole lot of nose to this import, but what there is turns out to be clean and outdoorsy. In the mouth the wine is very light in body, dry, and with an attractive if somewhat slender flavor. Better than average, but not enormously so. Price range: 24 oz, $1.39–2.39.

B & G CÔTES DU LUBERON   Bottled by Barton & Guestier, Blanquefort, France. Rating: 7+. Distribution: A. There's a touch of hot weather in the otherwise presentable nose of this transparent red import. There's also a slight briery component that is rather attractive, so maybe one cancels the other out. Performance in the mouth is middling. The wine is somewhat simple, thin, dryish, tart, but for all of it, refreshing. Price range: 24 oz., $1.99–2.49.

♀♀♀♀ B & G CÔTES DU RHÔNE   Bottled by Barton & Guestier, Beaune, France. Rating: 11+. Distribution: A. The color is a cool, transparent red. The aroma is racy and bracing, aromatic with spice and fruit and a lovely outdoorsy, woodsy feeling. There's plenty of fruit and spice in the taste, too, together with a crisp sprightliness, a nervy, peppery style that makes the wine a great delight. I think you'll find the whole experience stimulating and enjoyable, and if you don't, please send the rest of the bottle to me! Price range: 24 oz, $2.85–3.29.

♀♀♀ B & G DOMAINE DE LA MEYNARDE CÔTES DU RHÔNE Bottled by Barton & Guestier, Beaune, France. Rating: 10. Distribution: A. This is a wine full of energy and sunshine. The color is a light red, the nose is spicy and piquant, lively and fruity. The taste is equally sprightly; it's dry, the spice that the nose detected comes through in the mouth, and the light, energetic personality keeps right on giving. Price range: 24 oz, $2.49–3.19.

ΨΨ B & G PONTET-LATOUR BORDEAUX RED WINE Bottled by Barton & Guestier, Gironde, France. Rating: 9+. Distribution: A. This noble-sounding import is on the light side of medium red. The nose is simple, one dimensional, and unexciting. In the mouth the wine is dry, crisp, and pleasing, though void of force or dimension. Still, it has a touch of class, and it's worth your trying. Price range: 24 oz, $2.99–3.19.

ΨΨ B & G VIN DE CORBIÉRES Bottled by Barton & Guestier, Blanquefort, Gironde, France. Rating: 9+. Distribution: A. Color: lightish red, heading off in the direction of orange. Nose: clean, honest, shy. Taste: very light bodied, dry, and zesty. There's a nice showing of fruit, and a cheerfully spicy backdrop against which to view it. I like the wine, and have a feeling that there's something delightfully wicked about it, as though it might be a wine for well-to-do gypsies. Price range: 24 oz, $1.39–2.39.

ΨΨΨ RENÉ BARBIER TINTO Produced & bottled by René Barbier, San Sadurní de Noya (Panadés), Spain. Rating: 11. Distribution: C. René Barbier is one of Spain's well-known vintners, and this wine is robust, clean, refreshing, with a touch of spice in its flavor. The nose is friendly and pleasant, and everything about the wine is authentically Spanish. It's a classy wine, especially at the price, and an enjoyable experience. Price range: 24 oz, $2.25–2.55.

♀♀♀♀♀ BEAULIEU VINEYARD NAPA VALLEY BURGUNDY
Produced and bottled by Beaulieu Vineyard, Rutherford, California. Rating: 14. Distribution: B. This
Burgundy may well be the best in the price category.
My notes read: "Nose fantastic, rich, ripe, fruity,
deep, charming, expansive, rounded, bursting with
aroma, heady! Tastes joyous, full of life, full of fruit,
made with dash and style." You may gather from this
that I think Beaulieu's Burgundy is something you will
like. I do, I do! Price range: 25.6 oz, $2.99–3.19.

♀♀ BERINGER CALIFORNIA BARENBLUT Made and bottled by Beringer/Los Hermanos Vineyards, St. Helena, California. Rating: 9. Distribution: A. The color is
on the light side. There's fruit in the nose, but there's
also a slight dankness. In the mouth the wine is dry,
clean, and enjoyable, although somewhat thin.
Though not remarkable, a very attractive, enjoyable
wine. Price range: 25.6 oz, $2.75–2.99.

♀♀♀ BERINGER CALIFORNIA GRIGNOLINO Produced and
bottled by Beringer/Los Hermanos Vineyards, St.
Helena, California. Rating: 10. Distribution: A. This
pleasant red wine is the color of ripe strawberries. The
nose is clean and fruity, with touches of spiciness, and
the spice carries over into the mouth, where the effect
is peppery, fruity, unusual, and very pleasant. I think
it's a dandy wine. Maybe you will, too. Price range:
25.6 oz, $2.75–2.99.

♀♀ BERINGER CALIFORNIA ZINFANDEL Produced and
bottled by Beringer/Los Hermanos Vineyards, St.
Helena, California. Rating: 9+. Distribution: A. This

is a dark, rich-looking wine with orange tones. The nose is a little somber and briery, but not at all unpleasant. The taste is also a bit austere, with a nice balance of fruit and acid providing an agreeable combination of flavor and refreshment. It's a somewhat thoughtful wine, not terribly jolly, but who wants to be jolly all the time? Price range: 25.6 oz, $2.29–2.75.

ΨΨΨ BERINGER NORTH COAST BURGUNDY   Made and bottled by Beringer/Los Hermanos Vineyards, St. Helena, California. Rating: 10+. Distribution: A. This is one of the nice ones. A handsome red wine with hints of orange, a clean, fruity, sunshiny aroma, and a fresh, light-hearted taste, full of charm. Negatives? Well, I'd like it if the aroma had a little more assertiveness, but why quibble? It's plenty nice as it stands. Give it a try. Price range: 25.6 oz, $2.15–2.49.

ΨΨΨΨ BODEGA DE ORO PETITE SIRAH   Produced and bottled by Pacifico Tittarelli, Mendoza, Argentina. Rating: 11+. Distribution: C. This Argentine red has a lovely dark color, great body, good legs, and a strong, masculine, definitely upper-class aroma. It's medium dry, well balanced, fresh and charming, and I can't imagine how it came to be priced the way it is. It's a quality wine, dark and brooding, a wine for the dinner you plan to give for the prime minister. If you can find it at the right price, buy a case. Price range: 23.5 oz, $1.79–2.39.

ΨΨΨΨΨ BODEGA UNO CABERNET SAUVIGNON   Produced & bottled by Cooperativa Vitiv. La Consulta, Ltda, Mendoza, Argentina. Rating: 13. Distribution: C. From south of the equator comes a real winner! It has a bright, lively, red-orange color, and the nose is only the beginning of its show of class. It's full of fruit and briers, it's smooth, it's quiet, it's outdoorsy. The taste is dry, velvety, clean limbed, and you get a feeling of good bloodlines, maturity, and refinement. As you can see, I like it a lot, and I think you will, too. Price range: 23.5 oz, $2.49–2.99.

🍷🍷🍷 BOORDY VINEYARDS PINARD Produced and bottled by Boordy Vineyards, Penn Yan, New York. Rating: 11. Distribution: C. New York state has produced a charming wine in Boordy's Pinard. It has faint touches of orange in its color, and in the nose I seem to detect a touch of greenness among the flowers and fruit. It's a complex nose, with various layers to be sensed and evaluated, and it predicts the taste, which turns out to be light, fresh, and full of fruit and sunshine. It's a wine with charm and class. Price range: 25.6 oz, $1.89–2.19.

🍷 BOORDY VINEYARDS RED WINE Produced & bottled by Boordy Vineyards, Penn Yan, New York. Rating: 8. Distribution: C. This is a very decent wine that you will probably enjoy, even though it may seem to you, as it does to me, a stranger. The color is medium red, the nose is fair to middling with just a touch of stuffiness, as though no one at the winery ever opened the windows. In the mouth it has an unusual, interesting, and enjoyable flavor, as though the wine were made—and well made—from unfamiliar raw materials. Still, very pleasant. Price range: 25.6 oz, $1.89–2.39.

BRONCO CALIFORNIA BURGUNDY   Cellared & bottled by Bronco Winery, Ceres, California. Rating: 5+. Distribution: C. The wide-mouth carafe-type bottle is attractive enough, but the wine itself has a sharp, unpleasant odor that may be enough to keep you from trying its common, candy-box flavor. Price range: 32 oz, $.99–1.19.

♀ BRONCO CALIFORNIA CABERNET SAUVIGNON   Cellared & bottled by JFJ Winery, Ceres, California. Rating: 8. Distribution: C. This crimson Cabernet has an unexceptional but clean, rounded, and slightly sweetish aroma. In the mouth it's a bit thin and soda poppy, but you still get a certain amount of enjoyable fruit in the taste. It's somewhat rough, but then I never promised you a rose garden every time. Price range: 32 oz, $.99–1.29.

♀♀♀ CC VINEYARD CALIFORNIA BURGUNDY   Cellared & bottled by CC Vineyard Winery, Ceres, California. Rating: 11. Distribution: C. Here's a real sleeper! It's a Burgundy that costs little and delivers plenty! It's a slightly dense purple-red in color, and the nose is fresh, assertive, fruity, and has some very classy touches. The taste is moderately dry, cheerfully fruity, with a sunny open flavor and the pleasant surprise of finding this quality in a jug! Enjoy before it changes! Price range: 132 oz, $2.19–2.49.

CAMBIASO CALIFORNIA BURGUNDY   Made & bottled by Cambiaso Winery & Vineyards, Healdsburg, California. Rating: 7. Distribution: C. The aroma of this light-colored Burgundy is not unpleasant, but it's not quite pleasant, either! The wine is dry, a bit thin in body, and has a slight aftertaste it could do without. Thus, it's not a wine to write home about, but if you're offered it with your midweek dinner, don't turn it down! Price range: 25.6 oz, $1.59–1.79.

♀♀♀ CAMBIASO CALIFORNIA PETITE SIRAH   Made & bottled by Cambiaso Winery & Vineyards, Healdsburg, California. Rating: 11. Distribution: C. You'll like the deep, rich scarlet color of this wine, and you'll like what follows when you apply your nose and mouth to it. The nose is sedate and pleasing, with some refinement and no defects, and in the mouth the sensation is one of restraint and maturity, adult energy well under control. It's clean and honest, dignified, and it has character. It's a wine to *think* about as you drink it, and you ought to give it a try. Price range: 25.6 oz, $2.00–2.29.

CAMBIASO CALIFORNIA ZINFANDEL   Made & bottled by Cambiaso Winery & Vineyards, Healdsburg, California. Rating: 6. Distribution: C. This Zinfandel has no major faults, and no particular virtues. It's a little rough, has a slightly bitter aftertaste, but it also has some fruit showing through. The aroma is characterless and tired, but it's not offensive. It's just another wine. Price range: 25.6 oz, $2.00–2.29.

CAPPELLA RED TABLE WINE   Produced & bottled by Cappella Wineries, San Francisco, California. Rating: 7+. Distribution: B. The nose is slightly unripe, but not objectionably so. There are tinges of sweetness in the taste of this tart, berry wine, and the total picture is one of simplicity and cordiality. It's a little rough, but not enough to keep it from being a decent *vin ordinaire*. Price range: 25.6 oz, $1.19–1.59.

CARLO ROSSI'S RED MOUNTAIN CALIFORNIA BURGUNDY Made & bottled by Carlo Rossi Vineyards, Modesto, California. Rating: 7. Distribution: A. This is a simple, one-dimensional wine that seems devoid of any kind of excitement. It makes me think of a toy wine, the kind dolls might drink. It's red, it has some sweetness and some acid, but it's just terribly, terribly simple and ordinary. Nothing wrong with it, but nothing much going for it, either. Price range: 25.4 oz, $.99–1.25.

♀ CARLO ROSSI'S RED MOUNTAIN CALIFORNIA LIGHT CHIANTI Made & bottled by Carlo Rossi Vineyards, Modesto, California. Rating: 8. Distribution: A. This Chianti has a transparent scarlet color and a simple, sweetish, acceptable nose. The taste is also simple, clean, on the sweet side, but friendly and refreshing in a very unaffected way. It's not a wine of great character, but a little simplicity goes down very nicely every now and then. Price range: 25.4 oz, $.99–1.25.

♀♀♀ CARMEL ADOM ATIC Produced & bottled by Carmel Wine Growers Cooperative, Richon le Zion, Zichron Jacob, Israel. Rating: 10. Distribution: A. This is a very pleasing wine. You wouldn't call it stylish, because it isn't, but it has a sort of "very nice folks" character that makes it quite attractive. The nose is small but amiable, displays some fruit rather nicely, and the taste is semidry, straightforward, uncomplicated, and satisfying. Try it. Price range: 25.6 oz, $2.05–2.49.

♀♀♀ CASTILLO ARDAU RED TABLE WINE Bottled by Ardau, S.A., Areta-Llodio, Spain. Rating: 10. Distribution: C. This Spanish red has a rich ruby color and good body. The nose is enjoyably aggressive and slightly spicy, and the taste is dry, smooth, definitely Spanish, and very refreshing. Don't expect it to taste like a wine from California or France, because it has its own special taste and charm of a kind that seems to come only from the Iberian peninsula. Price range: 24 oz, $1.39–1.79.

♀♀♀♀ CHANSON CÔTES DU RHÔNE Produced & bottled by Chanson Père & Fils, Beaune, France. Rating 11+. Distribution: A. Nice! A rich, ruby color and an intrusive nose that has dignity, fullness, and style. Conservative style, nothing flashy. And the taste: dignity, quality, reserve, but at the same time, freshness. The fruit is there, and it is fully matured, almost to the point of being overripe. Nice, and I think you'll like it a lot! Price range: 24 oz, $2.69–2.99.

♀ CHÂTEAU DE ST. FERRÉOL RED WINE Produced & bottled by Perret of Mâcon, France. Rating: 8. Distribution: C. This pleasant French import promises a bit more than it delivers. Yet it has qualities that make it worth your trying it. The color is on the dark side of medium, the nose is sound and straightforward without offering anything you need to exclaim over. In the mouth it is dry, astringent, but still a good candidate to serve with some kinds of meals. It could be smoother; it's not what you would call distinguished. But it's interesting, and worth trying at least one bottle. Price range: 24 oz, $1.39–1.99.

CHÂTEAU TIMBERLAY BORDEAUX SUPÉRIEUR Mis en bouteilles au Château, R. Girard, propriétaire, Bordeaux, France. Rating: 7. Distribution: C. This wine has a lovely, deep color and an unfortunate slightly acrid nose. It's not awful, but just not terribly pleasant. The same rank flavor comes through in the wine itself, and although it improves with breathing, it's still a little too harsh and astringent to be a bargain at its price. Too bad. Price range: 24 oz, $2.89–3.19.

CHÂTEAU VIN BURGUNDY Produced by Lodi Vintners, Bottled by Carnot Vintners, Acampo, California. Rating: 7+. Distribution: C. This inexpensive wine has a handsome red color and an ordinary nose, mostly decent but with a faint fetid whiff that has to be called a defect. Nonetheless, it's not bad in the mouth. It has some sweetness that is moderately well compensated, and it's the kind of wine you can gulp with simple, hearty meals and enjoy it quite a bit. Price range: 25.6 oz, $.99–1.19.

ΩΩΩΩ CHRISTIAN BROTHERS SELECT CALIFORNIA BURGUNDY Produced & bottled by The Christian Brothers, Napa, California. Rating: 11+. Distribution: A. The color is reddish orange, the nose is forthright and assertive, and shows class. It's a mature-fruit bouquet, smooth and integrated. In the mouth the wine is pleasantly dry and tart, fresh and at the same time authoritative. I get a feeling of vigor and youth, and excellent family connections. Try it and see if you agree. Price range: 25.4 oz, $2.15–2.45.

♀♀ COCHS, S.A. TARRAGONA WINE   Bottled & shipped by Cochs, S.A., Reus, Tarragona, Spain. Rating: 9+. Distribution: C. This wine is very light in color for a red. Could be it is intended to work as a rosé, which it could be, chilled, very handily. It's authentic Spanish in aroma and taste. The nose is pleasant and not at all reluctant, the taste is dry, spicy, and has a nice acid balance. If you don't like Spanish wines, you may not like it, but if you do like them, this is a bargain. Price range: 24 oz, $1.19–1.39.

♀ CONCANNON VINEYARD CALIFORNIA BURGUNDY Made & bottled by Concannon Vineyard, Livermore, California. Rating: 8+. Distribution: C. This medium-red wine has an acceptable nose that is "closed in" and slightly stuffy in spite of having a middling display of fruit. The taste has a yeoman-of-the-guard sturdiness, stolid rather than zesty, robust, and fruity, with a sort of healthy peasant maturity. Not a bad wine at all, just not a member of the nobility. Price range: 25.6 oz, $2.25–2.79.

♀ CONCHA Y TORO CHILEAN BURGUNDY   Produced & bottled by Viña Concha y Toro, Chile. Rating: 8. Distribution: C. The color of this import is dark and rich. The nose is heavy, almost stuffed, but not offensive. The taste is also very heavy, an unusual, closed-in taste with some weeds and some spice, interesting and foreign, pleasing in a rather strange way. For the price, you can't afford not to try it and make up your own mind! Price range: 23.5 oz, $.99–1.29.

♀♀♀ CRESTA BLANCA MENDOCINO GAMAY BEAUJOLAIS Made & bottled by Cresta Blanca Winery, San Francisco, California. Rating: 10. Distribution: B. The color is a lovely scarlet. The nose is rounded, dignified, and shows some aristocratic flashes along with some occasional hints of hot weather. The mouth performance is very dry, light, crisp, and puckery. It's an energetic wine, a vivacious friend to accompany you through a long, enjoyable lunch. (Isn't it lunchtime right now?) Price range: 25.6 oz, $2.75–3.19.

♀♀♀♀♀ CRESTA BLANCA MENDOCINO ZINFANDEL Made & bottled by Cresta Blanca Winery, San Francisco, California. Rating: 13+. Distribution: B. We have a winner, folks! It's a lovely, clear orange-red wine with a cultivated, mature nose that displays lots of clean, classical features. Even if you never taste it, you'll enjoy the bouquet. The flavor is full, rounded, and zesty, with a pleasingly tart edge and heaps of fruit. All the components are nicely integrated into the whole, and I think it's terrific! Price range: 25.6 oz, $2.75–3.19.

CRESTA BLANCA NORTH COAST CALIFORNIA BURGUNDY Made & bottled by Cresta Blanca Winery, San Francisco, California. Rating: 7+. Distribution: B. The color is rich and dark, the nose is heavy, a bit lacking in class, but presentable. The taste is light, fruity, with a sweet-sour tartness and more astringency than I'd like, but still, the wine is decent if unremarkable. Price range: 25.6 oz, $1.99–2.49.

♀♀ FAMIGLIA CRIBARI CALIFORNIA CABERNET SAUVIGNON
Produced & bottled by B. Cribari & Sons, San Francisco. Rating: 9. Distribution: A. This is a good-looking wine with an ingratiating nose—rounded, fruity, developed, and with a hint of vanilla extract. In the mouth it displays the true character of the Cabernet grape. It's assertive, moderately dry, dignified, and refreshing in its balance. I wouldn't call it aristocratic, but it *is* authoritative, and I think you'll like it. Price range: 25.4 oz, $1.69–2.09.

FAMIGLIA CRIBARI CALIFORNIA MELLO BURGUNDY   Made & bottled by B. Cribari & Sons, San Francisco, California. Rating: 5. Distribution: A. This Burgundy is on the dark side of medium red. The nose is harsh, reedy, and processed. The mouth sensation is the same, bitter and not very pleasant. So it goes. Price range: 25.4 oz, $1.29–1.49.

♀ FAMIGLIA CRIBARI CALIFORNIA VINO ROSSO DA PRANZO
Made & bottled by B. Cribari & Sons, San Francisco, California. Rating: 8. Distribution: A. This is a clean, darkish, handsome wine with a simple, fruity, and not terribly exciting nose. There's nice fruit in the taste, with a supple, straightforward, very decent flavor. It's not a remarkable wine by any means, but it's cheerful and drinkable. Price range: 25.4 oz, $1.29–1.49.

♀ FAMIGLIA CRIBARI ZINFANDEL   Made & bottled by B. Cribari & Sons, San Francisco, California. Rating: 8. Distribution: A. I started buying Cribari wines a long time ago, principally because I liked the picture of Grandpa Cribari on the label. I buy Cribari's Zinfandel nowadays from time to time because it's a simple, direct, no-foolin' wine that's semidry and delivers a lot of fruit and refreshment at a modest price. A good, peasant wine, and I'm a peasant. Price range: 25.4 oz, $1.39–1.69.

♀ DANTE CHIANTI   Bottled by Dante, s.r.l., Terriciola, Toscana, Italy. Rating: 8+. Distribution: C. This Italian import has a zesty, grassy nose with a slightly sharp edge. The flavor is dry, nervy, and has a tinge of weediness. It's pleasant, different, and Italian, and worth a try if you can find a bottle at the right price. Price range: 24 oz, $1.09–1.79.

DELAVIN MONASTREL   Produced & bottled by Aquila Rossa, S.A., Vilafranca del Panadés, Spain. Rating: 6+. Distribution: C. The aroma is woody and weedy, the taste is earthy, rough, dry, and individual without being in any way endearing. Throw in a rather unfortunate aftertaste, and you haven't got much. Price range: 24 oz, $1.59–1.79.

♀♀♀ DELICATO ESPECIALLY SELECTED CALIFORNIA BURGUN- DY   Produced & bottled by Delicato Vineyards, Man- teca, California. Rating: 10+. Distribution: B. It seems to me that this wine is more like a Bordeaux than a Burgundy. The nose is somber but stylish, and there's a sort of Cabernet weediness in it. The taste is dry, classic, angular, and I get a feeling of matured fruit, and of grapes that may be of a higher quality than the low bottle price indicates. Price range: 25.6 oz, $1.39–1.59.

DELICATO ESPECIALLY SELECTED CALIFORNIA CABERNET SAUVIGNON: Made & bottled by Delicato Vineyards,

Manteca, California. Rating: 7+. Distribution: B. The color is on the dark side of medium red, and the nose is on the musty side of moderately acceptable. It's a bit rough in the mouth, the slight off-odor coming through in the taste. Not terrible, but nothing to spend any time seeking out in the stores. Price range: 25.6 oz, $2.69–3.19.

DELICATO ESPECIALLY SELECTED CALIFORNIA CHIANTI
Produced & bottled by Delicato Vineyards, Manteca, California. Rating: 7+. Distribution: B. The nose and taste of this Chianti make me think of a wet cellar. They're not awful, just a little musty and stale. There's fruit, there are some beginnings of character, but it's not enough to lift the wine out of the ordinary. Price range: 25.6 oz, $1.39–1.59.

DELICATO ESPECIALLY SELECTED CALIFORNIA CLARET
Produced & bottled by Delicato Vineyards, Manteca, California. Rating: 7+. Distribution: B. Delicato's Claret isn't wonderful, and it's not awful. It's just another wine that smells and tastes as though it was made in a laundry room where they never opened the windows. A bit swampy in the nose, a bit common and boring in the mouth. Just another wine. Price range: 25.6 oz, $1.39–1.59.

♀♀♀ DELOR MERLOT GRAND VIN DE BORDEAUX Shipped by A. Delor & Cie., Gironde, France. Rating: 10. Distribution: C. This is a good-looking wine on the light side of medium red. The nose is pleasing, forthright, vigorous, and speaks of fruit, brambles, and briers. In the mouth the wine has a light body, and is brisk, dignified in a lean, spare sort of way, refreshing, and pleasantly tart. If you can find it, it's a good buy. Price range: 24 oz, $1.99–2.49.

ϘϘϘ ECU ROYAL CLARET RESERVE   Shipped by Dulong Frères et Fils, Bordeaux, France. Rating: 10+. Distribution: B. This bulk import—it comes in gallons, half-gallons, and 1.5-liter bottles—has a pleasing, full, assertive nose that is clean and outdoorsy. The taste is moderately dry, bright, youthful, and refreshing, with an attractive roundness, and plenty of fruit in a congenial, slightly tart setting. Try it. Price range: 50.7 oz, $3.99–4.29.

ϘϘ EDEN VALLEY HERMITAGE   Vintaged & bottled by B.V.W. Pty, Ltd., Nuriootpa, South Australia. Rating: 9+. Distribution: C. This red wine from Australia has a bit of austerity and stand-offishness about it, but it's still a quality wine, a wine with true character. There's a touch of spiciness in the nose, and the taste is inviting and dry. Like the nose, there are touches of spice in the taste. The whole effect is of a refreshing but slightly reserved wine, and a wine you'll probably enjoy trying, if you can find it. Price range: 24 oz, $1.59–2.39.

ϘϘϘϘ FETZER VINEYARDS LAKE COUNTY ZINFANDEL   Produced & bottled by Fetzer Vineyards, Redwood Valley, California. Rating: 11+. Distribution: C. Fetzer has produced a deep, dusky scarlet wine with a round, mellow nose built along classic lines. There's a charming sense of wilderness in the taste—it's full, fruity, and has a verve and vigor that are very appealing. It's slightly astringent, and there's a certain amount of complexity to the whole design. So . . . find some, try some. Price range: 25.4 oz, $2.50–2.99.

☿ FETZER VINEYARDS MENDOCINO PREMIUM RED   Cellared & bottled by Fetzer Vineyards, Redwood Valley, California. Rating: 8. Distribution: C. This rich-looking wine is on the dark side of medium red. The nose is unobjectionable, but delivers no particular message. The taste is dry, light, zesty, with a somewhat piquant flavor, a faint spiciness, and a quality I can only think to describe as a slight dustiness. That may not sound good, but it is not an unattractive quality, and the wine may please you quite a bit. So try it. Price range: 25.6 oz, $2.25–2.65.

☿ FOLONARI BARDOLINO   Produced & bottled by SPAL, Pastrengo, Italy. Rating: 8. Distribution: B. The color is medium red, the nose is modest, clean, and without any particular character. The taste is light and dry, with a sort of berry flavor that is rather appealing. The wine has enough tartness to give it a moderate vigor and to make it worth your while to try it if you happen across it. Price range: 67.6 oz, $3.79–4.19.

☿ FOLONARI VALPOLICELLA   Produced & bottled by SPAL, Pastrengo, Italy. Rating: 8. Distribution: B. The nose of this light red wine has very little to say. If you try hard, you might detect a faint spiciness. The taste is dryish, clean, decent, quietly sprightly, and the mouth confirms the faint spice that the nose suspected. A nice wine of no particular consequence, so go ahead and enjoy it. Price range: 67.6 oz, $3.79–4.19.

FOPPIANO CALIFORNIA BURGUNDY   Made & bottled by
L. Foppiano Co., Healdsburg, California. Rating: 6+.
Distribution: C. The middling nose seems slightly
baked, but not offensively so. The wine itself is dry,
aggressively astringent, and has a bitter tone that
keeps it from being really pleasant. The color, on the
other hand, is rich, dark, and handsome. Price range:
25.6 oz, $1.49–1.69.

♀ FOPPIANO CALIFORNIA ZINFANDEL   Made & bottled
by L. Foppiano Wine Company, Healdsburg, California. Rating: 8. Distribution: C. The color of this wine
is quite dark, as Zinfandels go. The nose is shy,
innocuous, and unremarkable, but shows no particular defects. In the mouth the wine is simple, enjoyable, unspectacular, thin, refreshing, and fruity. A
nice middle-of-the-road Zinfandel to accompany a
nice middle-of-the-week dinner. Price range: 25.6 oz,
$1.49–1.69.

FRANZIA CALIFORNIA BURGUNDY   Made & bottled by
Franzia Brothers, Ripon, California. Rating: 7+. Distribution: B. Franzia's Burgundy is a transparent,
crimson wine with a middling nose and a middling
taste. There are no particular defects and no particular
charms. It's on the sweet side, it shows fruit, but it
makes me think of fruit-flavored soda pop. It will
wash down a dinner very handily, but no one will ask,
"Hey, what's the name of this wine, I want to write it
down!" Price range: 25.4 oz, $.99–1.29.

FRANZIA CALIFORNIA ROBUST BURGUNDY   Made & bottled by Franzia Brothers, Ripon, California. Rating:
7+. Distribution: B. The color is the scarlet of grena-

diers. The nose is clumsy and reflects hot weather. The taste has some sweetness, is fruity and simple, and the total effect is sturdily in the middle of the road. Price range: 25.4 oz, $.99–1.29.

♀ FRATELLI LAMBRUSCO   Produced & bottled by Nando Cavalli & Figli, Scandiano Emilia, Italy. Rating: 8. Distribution: B. This wine has the typical deep purple color of the Lambrusco wine type, and it's very handsome indeed. The nose is somewhat somber and upright. There's some sense of mature fruit, and even a whisper of something like a Cabernet in its ancestry, which seems unlikely. In the mouth the wine is grapey and sweet in the Lambrusco manner, but with a touch of spice and herbal character to relieve it. It has good balance despite the sweetness, and if you like sweet wines, you will probably like this one quite a bit. Price range: 24 oz, $2.19–2.59.

♀♀ GALLO CALIFORNIA BARBERA   Vinted & cellared & bottled by Ernest & Julio Gallo, Modesto, California. Rating: 9. Distribution: A. The nose of this darkish, brooding wine is a bit ponderous but otherwise acceptable, and the sensation in the mouth is of a very dry, lively, almost puckery wine. For a highly seasoned dinner it would provide a very nice accompaniment, while it might be too astringent with less assertive foods. On balance, not bad. Price range: 25.6 oz, $1.69–2.19.

GALLO CALIFORNIA BURGUNDY   Made & bottled by Gallo Vineyards, Modesto, California. Rating: 7+. Distribution: A. The color is a vibrant, clear red. The nose is not great, not terrible, and seems to me to possess components both of fruit and processing. I get the same dual personality in the mouth—fruit and process—and if there were a little more of the former and a little less of the latter, I'd move it up a notch. As it is, it's a nice, middling wine. Price range: 25.4 oz, $1.29–1.69.

♀ GALLO CALIFORNIA HEARTY BURGUNDY   Made & bottled by Gallo Vineyards, Modesto, California. Rating: 8. Distribution: A. This Gallo wine has won praise from many critics, and that alone may be enough to make you want to try it. What I find is a pleasing, fruity wine with a slight sweet-sour tartness, a simple, unspectacular nose, not a whole lot to remember, but certainly nothing amiss. I think it's a very decent wine, but since the other wine writers wax more lyrical about it than I, I think you ought to form your own opinion. Price range: 25.4 oz, $1.39–1.79.

♀ GALLO CALIFORNIA RUBY CABERNET   Vinted & cellared & bottled by Gallo Vineyards, Modesto, California. Rating: 8+. Distribution: A. This dark varietal offers a weedy, assertive nose that vouches for the Cabernet relationship. It's potent and a bit one dimensional, but still rather pleasant. In the mouth the wine is a shade off dry, nicely fresh, and without any complexity whatever. At the price the Gallo brothers ask for it, you probably should give it a try. Price range: 25.4 oz, $1.69–2.19.

GALLO CALIFORNIA ZINFANDEL   Vinted & cellared & bottled by Ernest & Julio Gallo, Modesto, California. Rating: 7. Distribution: A. The nose is reluctant and unremarkable, and there's a hint of bitterness in the flavor. The whole thing seems kind of thin, flat, and soft drinky to me, so I can't recommend that you rush right out and buy some. Price range: 25.6 oz, $1.49–1.89.

♀ GANCIA VALPOLICELLA CLASSICO SUPERIORE Bottled by Figli Gancia & Cia, Canelli, Italy. Rating: 8. Distribution: B. This cheerful-looking red has an attractive if somewhat bashful nose that is light, dignified, and has touches of style. The taste is thin, dry, zesty, uncomplicated. An Italian wine, it would go well with Italian dinners, where its vigor and slightly restrained fruit would complement the seasonings. Price range: 24 oz, $2.89–3.29.

♀ GINJAL RED WINE Produced & bottled by Soc. Com. Theotonio Pereira, Lda., Lisbon, Portugal. Rating: 8. Distribution: C. This Portuguese red comes in a pottery bottle, the contents of which I think you'll like. The aroma is forthright and full of fruit, the color is rich and attractive, and the taste is dry, fresh, fruity, and enjoyable. I will grant you that the wine is a bit hard on the tongue, but that's a small price to pay for a wine as vigorous and enjoyable as this one. Price range: 24 oz, $1.69–1.99.

♀♀ GIUMARRA CLASSIC CALIFORNIA BURGUNDY Produced & bottled by Giumarra Vineyards, Edison, California. Rating: 9. Distribution: C. This is a semi-dry, tart, fruity wine that tastes good without being terribly remarkable. It has no single outstanding marvelous characteristic (in fact, the nose seems a trifle cooked), but it all seems to hang together quite well and make a much-better-than-average accompaniment to a meal. See for yourself. Price range: 25.6 oz, $1.59–2.25.

GOLD SEAL CONCORD RED　Made & bottled by Gold Seal, Hammondsport, New York. Rating: 5. Distribution: C. There are few New York State wines that fit our price strictures, so our nostrils are entitled to flare in anticipation whenever we locate one we can afford. The flaring is for naught in this case, however, as Gold Seal's good-looking, transparent red wine turns out to be very grapey and soda-pop-like in aroma, flat and sweet in the mouth. I suppose it could be a dessert wine or perhaps a sacramental wine, although I wouldn't much want to attend the church that served it. Price range: 25.6 oz, $1.69–2.19.

ȲȲȲȲ GOYENECHEA CABERNET SAUVIGNON　Produced & bottled by Goyenechea & Cia, Villa Atuel, Mendoza, Argentina. Rating: 12+. Distribution: X. Finding a wine like this is one of the rich rewards of being a wine hunter. The wine has a rich, dark, brooding color and a deep, complex, cultivated aroma. The flavor is rich and refined, mouth filling, and has exceptional smoothness. I tasted a bottle, then ran right back to buy a case. I can't imagine that the wine is widely available, but keep your eyes open, and pester your liquor dealer. Price range: 24 oz, $1.59–2.59.

ȲȲȲȲ GRÃO VASCO DÃO　Produced by Grão Vasco, Viseu, Portugal. Rating: 11+. Distribution: B. This dark, handsome wine comes from the Dão Valley in Portugal, and it's a splendid wine to have in your arsenal, or cellar, or whatever it is you have. The aroma is assertive, deep, pleasantly heavy, well developed. There is a touch of spice both in the nose and in the mouth, where the wine's liveliness and good balance combine with its dry, piquant flavor to produce a quality wine. I'm sure you'll find it both charming and satisfying. Price range: 25 oz, $1.99–2.99.

GROWERS CALIFORNIA BARBERA   Produced & bottled by California Growers Winery, San Francisco, California. Rating: 7+. Distribution: A. Acceptable but dull. The color is dark and handsome, but the nose is heavy and sweetish. In the mouth the wine lacks vigor, and you'll be reminded as much of a candy store as of a winery. Unexciting, a little flat, but still acceptable. Price range: 25.6 oz, $1.29–1.59.

♀ GROWERS CALIFORNIA BURGUNDY   Made & bottled by California Growers Winery, San Francisco, California. Rating: 8. Distribution: A. This royal red Burgundy has a very decent nose that says ripeness and maturity. The wine itself has a sweetness that could bother you but probably won't, since it's relieved by a moderate amount of acid. Price range: 25.6 oz, $.88–1.09.

GROWERS CALIFORNIA CABERNET SAUVIGNON   Made & bottled by California Growers Winery, San Francisco, California. Rating: 7+. Distribution: A. The color is medium red, on the scarlet side. The nose has true Cabernet character but is a bit reedy and harsh. The taste is similarly strident, as though the wine were trying too hard to prove itself a Cabernet. It's a Cabernet all right, but not one you'll want to make your Saturday-night special. Price range: 25.6 oz, $1.39–1.59.

GROWERS CALIFORNIA RUBY CABERNET Produced & bottled by California Growers Winery, San Francisco, California. Rating: 7+. Distribution: A. It's a lovely color, dark and velvety, but the nose is ordinary and sweetish. It's clean, but no great treat. The taste is also on the sweet side for this type of Cabernet, and although the whole thing isn't awful, it's hard to think of it as a serious wine. Price range: 25.6 oz, $1.29–1.59.

GROWERS CALIFORNIA ZINFANDEL   Produced & bottled by California Growers Winery, San Francisco, California. Rating: 7. Distribution: A. This nice-looking, medium-red wine has a simple but agreeable aroma, and a very simple, undistinguished flavor. It's not really sweet, yet it has a slightly candied character that makes it seem ordinary. Price range: 25.6 oz, $1.29–1.59.

GUASTI CALIFORNIA CABERNET SAUVIGNON Made & bottled by Guasti Vintners, Delano, California. Rating: 6+. Distribution: B. You'll find some true Cabernet weediness in the nose of this wine, but it's somewhat strident and musty. You'll taste fruit and detect hints of breeding, but somehow they haven't been brought together into a really enjoyable wine. It's too puckery, and it's too bad. Price range: 25.6 oz, $1.59–1.79.

GUILD CALIFORNIA VINO DA TAVOLA RED   Made & bottled by Guild Wineries, Lodi, California. Rating: 7+. Distribution: B. There's a slight orange cast to this deep, handsome wine. The nose is acceptable, but carries overtones of slightly rank, green weeds. The taste, too, is slightly grassy, not unpleasant. It's refreshing, it shows its fruit well, but it's just a little coarse. Don't let that keep you from trying it for yourself, however. Price range: 25.4 oz, $1.19–1.55.

♀♀ INGLENOOK CALIFORNIA NAVALLE BURGUNDY Produced & bottled by Inglenook Vineyards, San Francisco, California. Rating: 9. Distribution: A. The bouquet of this medium red wine is clean, decent, and unremarkable. It's the performance in the mouth that wins this wine its rating. It's dry, racy, vigorous, and offers some complexity in the ripe grape flavors that give it its attractiveness. Not one of your great wines, but you'll enjoy it. Price range: 25.4 oz, $1.99–2.29.

♀♀ INGLENOOK CALIFORNIA NAVALLE CLARET Produced & bottled by Inglenook Vineyards, San Francisco, California. Rating: 9. Distribution: A. This wine is the color of ripe, red cherries, a very handsome wine indeed. The nose is modest but pleasing, three dimensional, with a sense of mature fruit. These touches of class carry over into the taste to produce a rounded, semidry wine, attractively fruity—I thought I also tasted vanilla—and with some admirable restraint. Give it a try. Price range: 25.4 oz, $1.99–2.29.

♀ INGLENOOK CALIFORNIA NAVALLE RUBY CABERNET Produced & bottled by Inglenook Vineyards, San Francisco. Rating: 8+. Distribution: A. Inglenook's Ruby Cabernet has tones of purple in its dark, brooding look. The nose is a little harsh, but has the weedy Cabernet aroma that is characteristic. It has a straightforward, clean, and pleasing taste. It's not a complex wine by any means, but it's nice enough to enjoy midweek. Saturday night you may want something a bit more elegant. Price range: 25.4 oz, $1.99–2.29.

♀ INGLENOOK CALIFORNIA NAVALLE ZINFANDEL Produced & bottled by Inglenook Vineyards, San Francisco, California. Rating: 8+. Distribution: A. This Zinfandel is pleasant and simple without having any great distinction. There are spicy overtones in the bouquet, and the fruit comes through in the tasting. Still, it's a bit thin and a bit flat, so it doesn't win too many ribbons. Price range: 25.4 oz, $1.89–2.19.

♀♀♀♀ INGLENOOK NORTH COAST COUNTIES VINTAGE BURGUNDY Produced & bottled by Inglenook Vineyards, San Francisco, California. Rating: 12. Distribution: A. This deep, dark, brooding Burgundy displays a breadth and harmony that are a pleasure to behold. The bouquet is velvety and sophisticated, and promises matured fruit in the glass, a promise the wine keeps by being dry, smooth, refined, well balanced, and possessed of a masculine elegance. Price range: 25.4 oz, $2.50–2.89.

♀♀♀ ITALIAN SWISS COLONY CALIFORNIA BARBERA Produced & bottled by Italian Swiss Colony, Asti, California. Rating: 11. Distribution: A. This is a sleeper. It won't appeal to every palate, but a lot of people will find that its lovely ruby color and its robust, forthright nose will make them think of words like "backbone . . . character . . . hardy peasant stock . . ." In the mouth it's a bracing wine, sturdy and fresh with a slightly weedy, slightly briery framework that supports an animated wine. It could be the pride of a small village somewhere in Italy. I like it. Maybe you will, too. Price range: 25.6 oz, $1.49–1.79.

ITALIAN SWISS COLONY CALIFORNIA BURGUNDY Produced & bottled by Italian Swiss Colony, Asti, California. Rating: 7+. Distribution: A. This is a very simple wine with absolutely nothing to offend you except perhaps a bit of roughness in the mouth. Nevertheless, it has fruit in the nose and mouth, it's clean, it's refreshing to the point of having a fair bite. So why doesn't it score higher? Well, it's so simple it's almost simple-minded, and while you'll be glad to have it accompany a meal, you won't remember a thing. Price range: 25.6 oz, $1.39–1.69.

ITALIAN SWISS COLONY CALIFORNIA CABERNET SAUVIGNON Vinted & bottled by Italian Swiss Colony, Asti, California. Rating: 7+. Distribution: A. Low-cost varietals like this one offer the wine drinker a reasonable chance to sample a single type of grape, since at least 51 percent of the grapes in the wine must come from the variety named on the label. This wine has the authentic varietal nose—the Cabernet weediness— but not a great deal to go with it. The structure is too simple, the wine too young, brash, and uncomplicated to make this a real bargain. Price range: 25.6 oz, $1.69–1.89.

♀ ITALIAN SWISS COLONY CALIFORNIA CHIANTI Produced & bottled by Italian Swiss Colony, Asti, California. Rating: 8+. Distribution: A. The color is a bit on the light side with orange glints. The nose is common but acceptable, on the sweet side, nothing special. In the mouth it's very decent, nice and jolly, with lots of fruit, but a bit too sweet overall for my tastes. Price range: 25.6 oz, $1.39–1.59.

♀ ITALIAN SWISS COLONY CALIFORNIA RUBY CABERNET Vinted & bottled by Italian Swiss Colony, Asti, California. Rating: 8. Distribution: A. This varietal has a scarlet color and a sharp, single-minded nose to keep you reminded of the hybrid grape from which it comes. The sensation in the mouth is refreshing, in spite of being a bit on the rough side. All in all, it's a bit immature and uncultured, but there's a vigor and character to it that make it worth trying. It would probably go best with a highly seasoned meal. Price range: 25.6 oz, $1.49–1.79.

♀♀ ITALIAN SWISS COLONY CALIFORNIA ZINFANDEL Vinted & bottled by Italian Swiss Colony, Asti, California. Rating: 9+. Distribution: A. Here's a wine that offers good value—an inexpensive Zinfandel that has an inviting flavor and bouquet. The aroma has a little fruit, a little spice, and the taste is clean and perky. It has a good balance of fruit and acid, and maybe it was just me, but I thought I detected a hint of blackberry jam in the background. *Blackberry jam?* Better try it for yourself. Price range: 25.6 oz, $1.49–1.79.

♀♀♀ JOUVET CÔTES DU LUBERON   Produced & bottled by C. Jouvet & Cie, Beaune, France. Rating: 11. Distribution: B. If you can find some of this wine at the same price I did, buy it at once! This is a handsome scarlet wine with an honest, rounded, although not spectacular aroma, but whatever it may lack in the nose it makes up for in the mouth. The wine is smooth and refreshing, a fairly serious wine, moderately dry with a touch of elegance and a good finish. Find some right away! Price range: 24 oz, $1.49–2.59.

ꟼꟼꟼꟼ KORBEL CALIFORNIA BURGUNDY Made & bottled by F. Korbel & Bros., Guerneville, California. Rating: 11+. Distribution: B. This wine has a dark crimson color that looks very rich in the glass. The nose, though shy, is clean and rounded, and the taste is lovely, well balanced, full of fruit and vigor, with a pleasing tart edge that makes you feel it's very well organized, very bracing, and very well made. Price range: 25.4 oz, $2.25–2.65.

ꟼꟼ KORBEL CALIFORNIA ZINFANDEL Produced & bottled by F. Korbel & Bros., Guerneville, California. Rating: 9+. Distribution: B. This Zinfandel is a lovely, deep red. The nose has fruit and berries in it, and just a slight touch of closed windows. The taste is lovely, dry, sylvan, full of berry fruit and touches of spice, somewhat astringent, and full of zest, woods, rocks, rills, and healthy vigor. Price range: 25.6 oz, $2.75–3.25.

ꟼꟼꟼ CHARLES KRUG NAPA VALLEY VINTAGE BURGUNDY Produced & bottled by Charles Krug Winery, St. Helena, California. Rating: 10. Distribution: B. This is an engaging and unusual Burgundy. The aromatic nose delivers spice, herbs, and fruit, and the tasting confirms it all: ripe fruit in the brier patch. The wine is bright, lively, fresh, and invigorating. I suggest you give it a test-hop. Price range: 25.4 oz, $2.25–2.65.

CHARLES KRUG NAPA VALLEY CLARET Produced & bottled by Charles Krug Winery, St. Helena, California. Rating: 7+. Distribution: B. The only surprise this

wine offers is the fact that it isn't better than it is.
We've come to expect more from Charles Krug.
Nonetheless, this Claret, brilliant enough in the glass,
is a trifle sour and thin, with a nose that, while not
really offensive, does have a manufactured or processed touch to it. Price range: 25.4 oz, $2.25–2.65.

♀♀♀ CHARLES KRUG NAPA VALLEY GAMAY BEAUJOLAIS
Produced & bottled by Charles Krug Winery, St.
Helena, California. Rating: 10+. Distribution: B. This
is a very nice wine that seems a bit too patrician and
restrained to be a Gamay, but let me hasten to assure
you, that doesn't hurt drinking it one bit. The color is
royal scarlet, the nose is balanced on the fence
between Cabernet elegance and sturdy yeomanry. In
the mouth it's light, dry, and displays both energy
and intellect. It's a trace somber, despite having lots
of fruit, and it seems to be telling us that it has noble
relatives. Price range: 25.4 oz, $2.75–3.19.

♀ LA MANJA RED WINE   Produced & bottled by Garrig-
os, Valencia, Spain. Rating: 8. Distribution: C.
There's a slightly herbal quality to both the aroma and
the taste of this Spanish import. If you like it, you'll
call it spiciness. It's a rather stern wine, with no
hearts and flowers in either the smell or taste. It has a
modest astringency that is becoming, and it's another
one of those enjoyable foreign experiences, in case
foreign experiences are what you enjoy. Price range:
24 oz, $.99–1.19.

M. LAMONT CALIFORNIA BURGUNDY   Produced & bottled by M. LaMont Vineyards, LaMont, California.
Rating: 7. Distribution: B. This Burgundy has a deep,

smoky color that's very handsome. The nose is not so handsome, however, and while it's not actually unpleasant, it seems kind of thin and "upper register," and I get a feeling the wine has passed through old water pipes. The taste is dry, astringent, and despite the presence of a certain amount of fruit, seems coarse. Admissible, but hardly a winner. Price range: 25.4 oz, $1.69–1.99.

♀♀ M. LAMONT CALIFORNIA CABERNET Produced & bottled by M. LaMont Vineyards, LaMont, California. Rating: 9+. Distribution: B. M. LaMont's Cabernet is inky, dark, rich looking, and has a clear, rounded aroma that seems to me to have a faint whiff of licorice in it. In the mouth the wine is smooth, dry, pleasing, refreshing. It's not a big wine or a complex wine, but it's very nice, and you ought to give it a taste test yourself. Price range: 25.4 oz, $1.99–2.39.

♀♀ M. LAMONT CALIFORNIA ZINFANDEL Produced & bottled by M. LaMont Vineyards, LaMont, California. Rating: 9+. Distribution: B. This Zinfandel has a pleasing raspberry color, and a piquant, zesty aroma of the outdoors. The taste is dry, clean, sturdy, and displays fruit nicely balanced by acid. Give this one a try. Price range: 25.4 oz, $1.99–2.39.

♀♀♀ LEHAIM RED TABLE WINE Bottled by Clairsoleil, Marseille, France. Rating: 11. Distribution: X. Lehaim is an example of the good luck you can have if you shop around. It's a classy red wine that you may not find anywhere. I found it in only one store, and I'm glad I did: it's a clear, light-ruby-colored wine with nice body, a pleasant, fruity aroma, and a light, dry, well-balanced flavor. The cork says that it was bottled under the control of the Rabbinate of Paris, and some of the label is in Hebrew. More than that I can't tell you, except that if you see a bottle, grab it! Price: 24 oz, $1.79.

LINI LAMBRUSCO   Produced & bottled by Lini O. & Figli, Reggio Emilia, Italy. Rating: 7+. Distribution: B. This Lambrusco is a deep, vivid purple, and has a very grapey, or "foxy" nose. A grapey nose isn't the worst thing in the world, but most wine drinkers hope for a little more breadth or complexity. The taste is similarly sweet, grapey, and I also think I tasted cherries, strawberries, raspberries, and possibly passion fruit. Anyhow, it's sweet and fruity as all get out, and if it doesn't bring Welch's grape juice to your mind, I'll be surprised. Price range: 24 oz, $1.99–2.49.

LOPE DE VEGA CLARET   Elaborado 6 criado por La Vinicola Iberica, S.A., Tarragona, Spain. Rating: 6. Distribution: C. This Spanish wine will probably make someone from Tarragona homesick, but it's a bit too funky and woody for the likes of me. The nose has an unfortunate bitter quality, and the taste is too full of stalks and stems and other underbrush to make it worthwhile to search for its redeeming characteristics. Price range: 24 oz, $1.19–1.39.

♀ LOS HERMANOS CALIFORNIA BURGUNDY   Made & bottled by Los Hermanos Vineyards, St. Helena, California. Rating: 8. Distribution: A. This clear, scarlet wine has an acceptable if unremarkable nose, decent with a bit of fruit. The taste has a sort of sweet-sour tartness to its otherwise sweetish flavor, and it is this balance that makes it a moderately pleasing Burgundy. The fruit is aggreable if not noble, and it will do well as an accompaniment to a simple dinner. Price range: 50.7 oz, $2.99–3.49.

ΨΨΨ LOS HERMANOS CALIFORNIA GAMAY BEAUJO-LAIS Made & bottled by Los Hermanos Vineyards, St. Helena, California. Rating: 10+. Distribution: A. The nose is brash, racy, attractive, and the taste is full of fruit. There's some sweetness, and I guess it could use a bit more acid, but it's really quite a nice, clean, attractive wine, and I think you owe it to yourself to try it. Price range: 50.7 oz, $3.39–3.99.

Ψ LOS HERMANOS CALIFORNIA ZINFANDEL Made & bottled by Los Hermanos Vineyards, St. Helena, California. Rating: 8. Distribution: A. The color is on the light side, the aroma is reedy, fruity, outdoorsy. The wine appears to be balanced toward the acid side, which means that it is lively and refreshing, provided your tongue can stand it. There's a simple, sunny, fruity, berry quality to the wine that's appealing, and even if it isn't great, it's probably worth tasting at least once. Price range: 50.7 oz, $3.19–3.69.

ΨΨ HENRI MARCHANT LABRUSCA Made & bottled by Henri Marchant Wineries, Hammondsport, New York. Rating: 9+. Distribution: C. No, it's not a Lambrusco, it's a Labrusca. It has a pleasing transparent scarlet color, and the nose shows some fruit, not a whole lot of it, but it's acceptable and simple. The taste is sweet, rounded, fruity, and makes me think of Delaware Punch, which I like. So how did a wine like this score this high? Well, if you like this *type* of sweet wine, this is a good member of that tribe, and you'll probably enjoy it a lot. But chill it! Price range: 25 oz, $2.00–2.39.

MARQUÉS DEL LAGAR TINTO Produced & bottled by Bodegas Marqués del Lagar, Logroño, Spain. Rating: 7+. Distribution: C. There is a commonness about this wine that keeps it from getting off the ground. The color is a rich, handsome red, and the nose is clean, lively, and has genial quantities of fruit. The taste, however, is too odd, too astringent, too baked to make it very charming. The taste has a sort of perfume quality, as though the grapes were grown in a Persian garden, but the negative qualities of the wine overpower it. Price range: 24 oz, $1.99–2.39.

♀ LOUIS M. MARTINI CALIFORNIA BURGUNDY Prepared & bottled by Louis M. Martini, St. Helena, California. Rating: 8+. Distribution: B. This Burgundy has a deep, inky color that in my youth we would have labeled "black cherry." The nose is clean, sturdy, masculine, and has a sort of somber fruitiness. In the mouth the wine is dry, a bit more biting than I would like, but still and all it's clean and pleasant and worth a try. Price range: 25.6 oz, $2.25–2.69.

♀♀♀♀ LOUIS M. MARTINI CALIFORNIA MOUNTAIN CHIANTI Prepared & bottled by Louis M. Martini, St. Helena, California. Rating: 11+. Distribution: B. Scarlet color, fresh, energetic, fruity nose with a touch of spice. Clean, lean, athletic taste, honest but unsophisticated, simple but sturdy and bracing. I think it's a fine wine, well made, genial and inviting, but don't expect complexity. Who needs complexity anyhow? Price range: 25.6 oz, $2.25–2.69.

♀ LOUIS M. MARTINI CALIFORNIA MOUNTAIN CLAR-
ET Prepared & bottled by Louis M. Martini, St.
Helena, California. Rating: 8. Distribution: B. The
fact that I once had lunch with the late, great Louis
Martini predisposes me to like all his wines. In blind
tasting, therefore, I was disappointed to find that this
Claret didn't rate higher. The nose was very ordinary,
and while the wine was pleasant and refreshing, it,
too, seemed light, thin, and ordinary. So it goes. Price
range: 25.6 oz, $2.25–2.69.

♀♀♀ LOUIS M. MARTINI CALIFORNIA MOUNTAIN RED WINE
Prepared & bottled by Louis M. Martini, St. Helena,
California. Rating: 10. Distribution: B. The color is
pleasing, the nose is pleasing, the taste is pleasing.
The color is a purply red, the nose is clean and
amiable and fruity. If you try very hard, you'll pick up
a faint touch of spice. The taste is lively, dry, spicy,
with a nice tart edge. It's a brash, ingratiating wine,
with lots of fruit, and you ought to get a bottle. Price
range: 25.6 oz, $1.75–2.39.

♀♀♀ LOUIS M. MARTINI CALIFORNIA ZINFANDEL Produced & bottled by Louis M. Martini, St. Helena,
California. Rating: 10+. Distribution: B. This is not a
particularly complicated wine, but it's a very pleasant
one. The color is strong and clean, and the bouquet
offers an enjoyable mixture of spice and berries. It's
refreshing in the mouth, well balanced, with plenty of
ripe fruit, and the sum total of all this is that you
should rush right out and buy some. Price range: 25.6
oz, $2.75–3.29.

♀ MASCARA RED TABLE WINE Imported from Algeria,
North Africa, bottled by Vermat, Inc., Thibodaux,

Louisiana. Rating: 8. Distribution: C. The price is an enormous attraction in looking at this import, and amazingly, it has a few classy touches. The color is dark, almost murky, the nose is round, a bit oldish, a bit baked. The same hot weather turns up in the taste, but there's enough depth, smoothness, and generosity in the flavor to keep things interesting. At the price, you can't afford not to try it. Price range: 25.6 oz, $.89–1.09.

ΨΨ PAUL MASSON BAROQUE Made & bottled by Paul Masson Vineyards, Saratoga, California: Rating: 9+. Distribution: A. Baroque is Paul Masson's brand name, so nobody else will be offering you a Baroque. This one is a dark, brooding wine, somewhat austere and oldish in its bouquet. There's a certain richness and smoothness in the taste of the wine, however, a good balance of fruit sugar and acid, and when you're feeling austere and dignified, you'd better stroll on down and get a bottle. I think you'll like it. Price range: 25.4 oz, $2.09–2.49.

PAUL MASSON CALIFORNIA BARBERA Produced & bottled by Paul Masson Vineyards, Saratoga, California. Rating: 7. Distribution: A. Not Paul Masson's best effort. A lighter-than-average Barbera color and a somewhat fatigued nose with petroleum overtones. The same tones appear in the mouth. Not wonderful. Price range: 25.4 oz, $2.29–2.49.

Ψ PAUL MASSON CALIFORNIA BURGUNDY Made & bottled by Paul Masson Vineyards, Saratoga, California. Rating: 8+. Distribution: A. It's a good-looking, medium-red Burgundy with orange tones. The nose is adequate—that is, half the time it seems a bit baked, and the other half it seems to be trying to project some notes of austere quality. In the mouth it's similarly austere, not a fun-and-games type of Burgundy, but one that will cause you to think a bit. It's dry, astringent, won't please everyone, and it's definitely not for sissies. Price range: 25.4 oz, $2.15–2.39.

♀♀ PAUL MASSON CALIFORNIA GAMAY BEAUJOLAIS Made & bottled by Paul Masson Vineyards, Saratoga, California. Rating: 9. Distribution: A. The color is rather light, clear, with hints of red-orange. The nose is shy, decent, and has a slight woodsy-weedy component. The taste is dry, light, cheerful, unassuming. The wine is modestly fruity and spicy, very clean cut, and I have the feeling I'm associating with the young, untitled cousin to the duke, but not the duke himself. Price range: 25.4 oz, $2.99–3.29.

♀ PAUL MASSON CALIFORNIA PETITE SIRAH Made & bottled by Paul Masson Vineyards, Saratoga, California. Rating: 8+. Distribution: A. This is a dark, brooding, purply-red wine with a piquant, aromatic nose. The aroma is slightly exotic, and has a brash fruitiness that says this isn't your ordinary bottle of wine. The taste is quite pleasant, but since it's a foreigner to many, not everyone will accept it right away. It has a slight greenness in the taste, a sort of grassiness that may turn some people away, but others will find it a very enjoyable sensation. Price range: 25.6 oz, $2.99–3.29.

♀♀ PAUL MASSON CALIFORNIA PINOT NOIR Made & bottled by Paul Masson Vineyards, Saratoga, California. Rating: 9+. Distribution: A. This is a very decent wine of medium-red color, with a touch of restraint, even stuffiness, in the otherwise presentable nose, and a dry, slightly thin, but very pleasing flavor, fresh and enjoyable. It's an adult wine, thoughtful and reserved, and it certainly deserves at least one sampling. Price range: 25.4 oz, $2.99–3.29.

♀ PAUL MASSON CALIFORNIA ZINFANDEL   Made & bottled by Paul Masson Vineyards, Saratoga, California. Rating: 8+. Distribution: A. "Decent" is the word that comes to mind. There are no technical defects, the wine is refreshing, balanced toward the acid side of things, and it all adds up to something pleasant but characterless. For the same money, you can do better. Price range: 25.4 oz, $2.59–2.79.

♀ PAUL MASSON RUBION   Made & bottled by Paul Masson Vineyards, Saratoga, California. Rating: 8. Distribution: A. The color is light red, the nose is a bit heavy and lacks finesse. The taste offers a sense of maturity and reserve. It's dry, light, and has a modicum of tartness sprinkled through the fruit. Some people wax more enthusiastic than I over this wine, so you'd better try it yourself. I like it, you may love it! Price range: 25.6 oz, $2.09–2.49.

MAZZOLINI BARBERA   Produced & bottled by Mazzolini Donato & Giuliano, Cingia de Botti, Italy. Rating: 7+. Distribution: C. This Barbera is sturdy and aggressively middle class. It's presentable, suit mended and pressed, hair combed, but that's about it. The nose is acceptable but dull, the taste has an acceptable sweet/dry tartness, and the whole thing, as I said, is acceptable, but devoid of any elements of excitement or class. Price range: 24 oz, $1.19–1.39.

MAZZOLINI LAMBRUSCO Produced and bottled by Mazzolini, Donato & Giuliano, Cremona, Italy. Rating: 6. Distribution: C. Lambrusco has become a popular wine in recent years, probably because it is sweet and semisparkling and romantic, etc. It's a good wine to chill thoroughly and drink after tennis on a hot day. This Mazzolini offering, I'm sorry to say, is not one of the better Lambruscos. The wine, clean and lovely to look at, is simply not clean to the nose or mouth. It is sweet, thin, common, and has overtones of the Great Dismal Swamp. Alas! Price range: 24 oz, $1.19–1.39.

♀♀♀ MIRASSOU SANTA CLARA BURGUNDY Produced & bottled by Mirassou Vineyards, San Jose, California. Rating: 10. Distribution: B. Mirassou's Burgundy is a full, rich red with orange overtones. The nose is decent and fruity, with a slight lack of freshness, the kind that reminds you of rooms where they never open the windows. In the mouth, however, the wine gives a sterling performance, honest and straightforward, rounded, well balanced, and . . . well, *settled*. It's fruity and mature and adult without being intellectual or anything very heavy, and it all adds up to a nice, solid, enjoyable wine. Price range: 25.6 oz, $2.75–3.19.

♀♀♀♀♀ MOMMESSIN CÔTES-DU-RHÔNE Shipped by Mommessin, Mâcon, France. Rating: 13+. Distribution: B. The color is brilliant and light. The nose is spicy and fresh, outdoorsy, charming, and full of berries and brambles. The taste is spice, dry fruit, tweed, brisk autumn days, tramps in the dry woods with a friend from Austria, an expensive shotgun, a brace of partridges. In short, it has vigor and class, and I think you'll enjoy it. Price range: 24 oz, $2.99–3.19.

♀♀♀ CK MONDAVI CALIFORNIA SELECT BARBERONE Made & bottled by C. Mondavi & Sons, St. Helena, California. Rating: 10. Distribution: A. The word "Barberone" means a big Barbera, and the description is apt. This darkish wine has the austerity and authority of a dignified peasant patriarch. The nose is honest, forthright, impressive in a simple, uncomplicated way. The wine tastes clean, neat, rounded, with honest fruit and a slightly stiff, masculine decency through the whole bottle. Price range: 25.4 oz, $1.59–1.89.

♀ CK MONDAVI CALIFORNIA SELECT BURGUNDY   Made & bottled by C. Mondavi & Sons, St. Helena, California. Rating: 8. Distribution: A. This is a very acceptable Burgundy, one you can serve without concern, but it seems to me to lack excitement. It has a middling bouquet, simple, with some fruit, and it's fresh and clean and fruity in the mouth. Still, despite these pleasing qualities, it's too subdued, and perhaps a little too simple, to win a higher rating. Price range: 25.4 oz, $1.59–1.89.

♀♀♀ CK MONDAVI CALIFORNIA SELECT CHIANTI   Made & bottled by C. Mondavi & Sons, St. Helena, California. Rating: 11. Distribution: A. There's a touch of orange in this brilliant red wine. The nose is robust, somber, dignified in a rustic way. The taste is hearty, refreshing, has sufficient fruit peeking through, and reminds me of white-haired old men, sitting ramrod straight in the sunshine in some Italian hill town, talking and drinking some of this wine. Give it a try! Price range: 25.4 oz, $1.59–1.89.

ΨΨΨ CK MONDAVI CALIFORNIA SELECT CLARET   Made & bottled by C. Mondavi & Sons, St. Helena, California. Rating: 10+. Distribution: A. This lovely scarlet wine has an animated, but dignified, bouquet. It's sturdy and a bit somber, but very nice. Similarly, the taste is dry, serious, even forceful, and shows good breeding and mature fruit. Like some other wines, I see it being drunk by wise old men who know which wines satisfy the intellect as well as the palate. Price range: 25.4 oz, $1.59–1.89.

ΨΨΨ CK MONDAVI CALIFORNIA SELECT ZINFANDEL   Made & bottled by C. Mondavi & Sons, St. Helena, California. Rating: 10. Distribution: A. There is an adult quality to this wine that makes it very satisfying. There are purply tones in the otherwise medium-red color, and the nose is clean, masculine, and has a sort of "settled" quality to it. In the mouth it's dry, fruity, has light body, some refinement, and you get a feeling of quiet vigor and character. I like it. Price range: 25.4 oz, $1.69–1.99.

ROBERT MONDAVI CALIFORNIA RED TABLE WINE   Produced & bottled by Robert Mondavi Winery, Oakville, California. Rating: 7. Distribution: A. There are handsome purple glints in Robert Mondavi's red table wine, but not a lot more that will excite you. The nose was not bad, but it made me think of musty, vacant rooms, and in my mouth it tasted oldish, sedentary, and lacking in excitement of any kind. The taste includes fruit, and the balance is good, but on the whole the wine seemed a bit thin and disappointing. Price range: 25.6 oz, $2.19–2.59.

♀ THE MONTEREY VINEYARD ZINFANDEL Produced & bottled by The Monterey Vineyard, Gonzales, California. Rating: 8+. Distribution: C. This Zinfandel is just one of the crowd—amiable, forgettable, undistinguished. The aroma is slightly candied, the wine itself is a bit thin, a bit lacking in acid balance, although the fruit does come through in a rather pleasant fashion. An okay wine, one of the crowd, but one that wouldn't be missed if absent. Price range: 25.6 oz, $2.99–3.49.

♀♀♀ NOVITIATE CALIFORNIA BURGUNDY Produced & bottled by Novitiate of Los Gatos, Los Gatos, California. Rating: 10. Distribution: C. There are warm orange tones in this handsome red wine. The nose seems to say that it has good bloodlines, while being a little stuffy. The taste is semidry, fruity, a bit on the restrained, austere side of things, masculine, and offering some depth. If this sounds ambiguous, let me say that it's a quality wine, and you ought to give it a try. Price range: 25.6 oz, $2.50–2.99.

♀ PAISANO Made & bottled by Gallo Vineyards, Modesto, California. Rating: 8. Distribution: A. There's nothing wrong with simplicity, and this wine proves it. It doesn't try to be a big-time circus performer, and instead chooses to be an honest, dependable laborer, worthy of his (or her) hire. The color is a light, clear red, the nose has no great virtues or defects, the taste is simple, ingratiating, fruity, uncomplicated, and enjoyable. If you're a peasant like me, there's a time for a wine like this. Price range: 25.4 oz, $1.19–1.59.

♀ PAMPAS TINTO   Produced & bottled by Bodegas y Viñedos Lopez, Mendoza, Argentina. Rating: 8+. Distribution: C. There's a touch of burnt orange in the color of this inexpensive import, and there's a touch of something earthy in the otherwise clean, forthright aroma that differentiates this wine from the average red. The same thing carries on into the mouth, where I found the wine pleasant but with a slight stemminess that lingered on into the finish. The wine is dry, dignified, and slightly astringent, but not everyone will like its character and restraint. The only way to find out is to try it. You won't be risking much money. Price range: 24 oz, $1.19–1.39.

♀♀♀♀ ANGELO PAPAGNI CALIFORNIA BARBERA   Cellared & bottled by Papagni Vineyards, Madera, California. Rating: 11+. Distribution: B. This is an exhilarating wine, dry, fresh, with a nice biting edge and some genial fruit subtleties. The nose is modest but pleasing, with a faint touch of spice, but it's the sensation in the mouth that makes it so appealing. Spice, briers, fruit, freshness, sturdiness, and more than a touch of class. Price range: 25.6 oz, $2.50–2.99.

♀♀ ANGELO PAPAGNI CALIFORNIA ZINFANDEL   Cellared & bottled by Papagni Vineyards, Madera, California. Rating: 9. Distribution: B. You'll need a spicy dish to accompany this energetic Zinfandel, because it's dry and astringent, full of zesty tartness. But, given the right accompaniment, you'll like the wine, because it has a clean, fresh, straightforward bouquet with the fruit nicely and simply making its highly agreeable statement. So, next time you have spaghetti and meatballs, have some of this with it. Price range: 25.6 oz, $2.50–2.99.

ΨΨΨ PARDUCCI CALIFORNIA VINTAGE BURGUNDY Produced & bottled by Parducci Wine Cellars, Ukiah, California. Rating: 10+. Distribution: B. The bouquet of this handsome, red wine is full, pleasing, rounded, and calls to mind mature fruit, and for me, overtones of vanilla. The taste is moderately dry, mild, gracious, friendly, with attractive fruit flavors and a genial acid balance. A nice wine, a good wine. Price range: 25.6 oz, $2.50–3.10.

PEDRONCELLI SONOMA COUNTY BURGUNDY Produced & bottled by J. Pedroncelli Winery, Geyserville, California. Rating: 6. Distribution: B. Not much here, I'm afraid, outside of its lovely scarlet color. The wine has a dank, unpleasant, laundry-room odor, and the taste is flat, common, and undistinguished. Price range: 25.6 oz, $2.00–2.49.

PEDRONCELLI SONOMA COUNTY ZINFANDEL Produced & bottled by J. Pedroncelli Winery, Geyserville, California. Rating: 5. Distribution: B. Alas, Pedroncelli's Zinfandel is rough and acidic with bitterness in the aftertaste. The aroma is stale and disagreeable, and this seems to be confirmed in the tasting. Too bad. Price range: 25.6 oz, $2.50–2.99.

♀ PEDRONCELLI SONOMA RED WINE Bottled by J. Pedroncelli Winery, Geyserville, California. Rating: 8+. Distribution: B. The color is almost bluish. The nose is simple, unprepossessing, and acceptable. The taste is light and dry, vigorous but puckery, fresh, and fruity. It's not one of your more cultivated wines, but it has charm, especially with a highly flavored Italian dinner. Price range: 25.6 oz, $1.59–1.79.

PETRI AMERICAN BURGUNDY Produced & bottled by Petri Wineries, San Francisco, California. Rating: 7+. Distribution: A. Petri's Burgundy is acceptable but ordinary. It has a fine color, but a run-of-the-mill nose. In the mouth it is slightly sweet and lacking in the acid that would make it a more appealing, more refreshing product. Price range: 25.6 oz, $.99–1.39.

♀♀ PETRI AMERICAN CHIANTI Produced & bottled by Petri Wineries, San Francisco, California. Rating: 9. Distribution: A. This Chianti is cheerful and tends to be a trifle on the sweet side. It has nice fruit in the taste, but the nose is ordinary and a bit tired. You would gladly overlook it, however, if you had just been served a big helping of lasagna and a brimming glass of this wine. Price range: 25.6 oz, $.99–1.39.

♀ RICASOLI BARDOLINO Produced & bottled by Cantina Sociale Valtramigna, Verona, Italy. Rating: 8+. Distribution: B. Tart? Wow. Dry? Almost to the point of sourness. Zesty, fruity, astringent? Yes, yes, yes. This good-looking wine, a medium red with tones of orange, is meant for dinners that sear the roof of your mouth with heat and spices. The nose? Decent, slightly baked, no big deal either way. A nice, vigorous wine, but not for everyone. Price range: 24 oz, $2.99–3.29.

RIUNITE LAMBRUSCO   Produced & bottled by Cantine Coop. Riunite, Reggio Emilia, Italy. Rating: 7+. Distribution: A. This wine is a deep, royal purple, and looks as though only kings should drink it. The nose is a bit aggressive and has a kind of green geranium component. Still, the nose is acceptable, if slightly synthetic. In the mouth the wine is sweet, flat, grapey, and synthetic, and reminds me of wild-cherry cough drops. I know there are many people who love the various Lambruscos, and those people may love this one. Price range: 24 oz, $2.39–2.59.

♀♀ ROCAFLOR MINERVOIS   Produced & bottled by Union des Caves du Canton de Ginestas (Aude) France. Rating: 9+. Distribution: C. It is said that in Roman times, the Tenth Legion took wine from the Minervois region back to Italy. Taste this bottle and you'll understand why. Although the aroma is somewhat reluctant, it comes through pleasantly enough if you give it time. The flavor—well, there is a spot on the fence directly halfway between sweet and dry, and that's where this wine sits. It won't shrivel your tonsils, and it won't cloy them, either. In short, this is a nice, modest, well-balanced wine, and I hope you can find it. Price range: 24 oz, $1.59–1.99.

SAN MARTIN CALIFORNIA CABERNET RUBY   Produced & bottled by San Martin Winery, San Martin, California. Rating: 7+. Distribution: B. This garnet-colored wine has a very decent, simple nose, and a tart, vociferous, fruity taste. Somehow, it lacks fullness, roundness, and class. It's an okay wine, but just not anything special. Price range: 25.6 oz, $2.50–2.99.

♀ SAN MARTIN MOUNTAIN BURGUNDY   Produced & bottled by San Martin Vineyards, San Martin, California. Rating: 8. Distribution: B. The color of this wine seems a little light for what we ordinarily think of as a Burgundy, but it's clear and handsome enough. The aroma is unextraordinary, average, acceptable. The flavor is pleasant, smooth, unexciting, a bit on the flat side. You certainly won't hate it; you may like it; and I think you'll agree that it's a sound wine, plain perhaps, but sound. Price range: 25.6 oz, $1.69–1.99.

♀♀♀♀ SAN MARTIN SANTA CLARA VALLEY BURGUNDY Produced & bottled by San Martin Vineyards, San Martin, California. Rating: 11+. Distribution: B. The color is a brilliant scarlet, the nose is zesty, bright, fruity, and has a genial freshness. The taste has some complexity and is full of berries and briers, tons of fruit, and has a pleasantly dry flavor that calls up open fields, sunshine, and sky. Price range: 25.6 oz, $2.25–2.75.

♀♀♀ SEBASTIANI NORTH COAST COUNTIES BURGUNDY Produced & bottled by Sebastiani Vineyards, Sonoma, California. Rating: 10+. Distribution: A. This is a rich, inky wine with a delightful nose that is rounded, cultured, and spicy. It undoubtedly sounds affected to say that it seems athletic, but I guess it's the sprightliness of the flavor, its freshness, its fruit, its agreeable dryness, and its clean finish. I get a nice, sunny vineyard feeling drinking it, and maybe you will, too. Price range: 25.4 oz, $2.30–2.59.

♀♀♀ SEBASTIANI NORTH COAST COUNTIES CHIANTI Produced & bottled by Sebastiani Vineyards, Sonoma, California. Rating: 10. Distribution: A. I like the dark, dusky color of this Chianti, and while the aroma isn't anything you'd exclaim about, it's decent enough in a slightly pungent way. The taste is what I like best about this wine—nice, clean flavors, refreshing, fruity, energetic, full bodied, and a very engaging personality. I hope you find you agree. Price range: 25.4 oz, $2.50–2.89.

♀♀♀♀ SEBASTIANI NORTHERN CALIFORNIA BURGUNDY Cellared & bottled by Sebastiani Vineyards, Sonoma, California. Rating: 11+. Distribution: A. This is a dark, handsome wine with a fully matured bouquet, soft and round, calling up thoughts of ripe grapes and craftsmanship. In the mouth it's dry, deep, velvety, serene, thoughtful. It's an adult wine, dispensing mature pleasure but not gaiety, and I think you'll like it a great deal. Price range: 25.4 oz, $1.60–1.79.

♀♀♀ SEBASTIANI NORTHERN CALIFORNIA MOUNTAIN CABERNET SAUVIGNON Made & bottled by Sebastiani Vineyards, Sonoma, California. Rating: 10+. Distribution: A. The aroma of this dark, smoky Cabernet is clean, mild, and authentic. There's some breadth to the taste, some fruit, some refreshment, some dignity. Give it a try. Price range: 25.4 oz, $2.59–2.89.

♀ SEBASTIANI ZINFANDEL Produced & bottled by Sebastiani Vineyards, Sonoma, California. Rating: 8+.

Distribution: A. "Unspectacular" is the word for this Zinfandel. The label talks about "bramble flavor," but mostly what I get out of it is a sweetish nose and a very ordinary, slightly flat sensation in the mouth. It's one of those "okay" wines, but you won't sit around the dinner table uttering happy little cries as you smell or taste it. Price range: 25.4 oz, $2.50–2.89.

SEGESTA MELLOW RED ITALIAN WINE Produced & bottled by Diego Rallo & Figli., Marsala, Italy. Rating: 6+. Distribution: B. This scarlet wine has a hot-weather nose and a whiff from the tire factory. Unfortunately, these characteristics carry over into the taste, with the result that the fruit can never come through the vulcanization barrier. Since it's a popular wine among many people of Italian descent, I can only assume that it is an acquired taste. Price range: 24 oz, $2.99–3.49.

♀♀♀ SETRAKIAN MOUNTAIN RED BURGUNDY Produced & bottled by Robert Setrakian Vineyards, Yettem, California. Rating: 11. Distribution: B. This is an exceptionally nice wine, a "find." Has a deep, rich color, decent body, and a good, clean nose that is not backward in making its presence known. It is smooth and full in the mouth, with a good finish and a touch of elegance overall. Your dinner guests will like it, and so will you. Price range: 25.6 oz, $1.39–1.69.

♀♀ SONOMA VINEYARDS SONOMA COUNTY GAMAY BEAUJO-LAIS Produced & bottled by Sonoma Vineyards, Windsor, California. Rating: 9+. Distribution: B. This is a light, amiable, simple wine that is pleasantly outdoorsy and fresh both in the nose and in the mouth. In color it's a pleasing crimson. The aroma is expansive and engaging, without complexity but without defects, either. There's plenty of fruit in the taste, there's plenty of refreshment in the acid balance, and I think you'll enjoy it. Price range: 25.4 oz, $2.99–3.35.

♈♈♈♈ SONOMA VINEYARDS ZINFANDEL   Produced & bottled by Sonoma Vineyards, Windsor, California. Rating: 11+. Distribution: B. Here it is, folks, one of the goodies. The color is handsome and brilliant, the nose is rich, deep, and beckoning, with some floral complexities that make the experience worthwhile before you ever get to the taste. The taste has the same sort of depth, with an enjoyable patina of fruit sugar and a sense of good breeding. So, if your bottle is like the bottles I tested, you're in for a treat! Price range: 25.4 oz, $2.59–3.19.

♈♈♈ SOUVERAIN OF ALEXANDER VALLEY NORTH COAST BURGUNDY   Produced & bottled by Souverain, Geyserville, California. Rating: 10+. Distribution: B. This dark, cherry-red wine has a soft, clean nose with a modest showing of fruit. The taste is dry, with medium body, a generous quantity of fruit, and a brash, nervy spiciness that gives it a lot of life. It's a wine with structure, a young, zesty, light-hearted wine built according to a good plan. The wine itself isn't intellectual, but the people who made it must have been. Price range: 25.6 oz, $2.50–2.99.

♈♈♈♈ SOUVERAIN OF ALEXANDER VALLEY SONOMA ZINFANDEL   Produced & bottled by Souverain, Geyserville, California. Rating: 11+. Distribution: B. This is a lovely wine. The nose is slender and clean, with ripe fruit and a dollop of vanilla extract in the bouquet. The taste is light, dry, nervy, with just the right amount of acid balance. I get a faint air of mystery in the wine, touches of fruit and musk, and the whole thing is woodsy and inviting. Price range: 25.6 oz, $2.75–3.29.

♀♀♀♀ STERLING NAPA VALLEY RED WINE Bottled by Sterling Vineyards, Calistoga, California. Rating: 11+. Distribution: B. Simplicity can be very charming, and this wine proves it. From its deep purply color to its fresh, clean, straightforward aroma and its fresh, clean taste, it's not complex, not fancy, and yet it's a very enjoyable wine. There's plenty of fruit in the modestly piquant nose, and tons more in the taste. There's a bit of astringency, if that kind of thing bothers you, but it's under control, and the whole thing adds up to a wine that's pleasant, supple, and very drinkable. Price range: 25.6 oz, $2.49–2.99.

♀ TAYLOR LAKE COUNTRY RED Produced & bottled by Taylor Wine Co., Hammondsport, New York. Rating: 8. Distribution: B. This wine is a bit too grapey and sweet for me, but that doesn't mean that you might not enjoy it. The color is a trace on the light side, the aroma is as simple and grapelike as the taste, and the total effect is on the sacramental side. Price range: 25.6 oz, $2.15–2.59.

♀♀♀♀♀ TORRES CORONAS Produced & bottled by Miguel Torres, Vilafranca del Panadés, Spain. Rating: 13. Distribution: B. A lovely wine! It has a deep garnet color, and a beautifully rounded nose of some mature complexity. It's aromatic, full of flowers and fruit. The taste has the attractive simplicity of natural good breeding. It's light, generous, rounded, refreshing, and makes me think of a beautiful afternoon spent outdoors under a big tree, talking with old friends. Don't miss it! Price range: 24 oz, $2.65–2.99.

ΨΨΨΨ TORRES SANGRE DE TORO   Produced & bottled by Miguel Torres, Vilafranca del Panadés, Spain. Rating: 12. Distribution: B. I don't believe you have to be an aficionado of Spanish wines to enjoy the power and vigor of this dark, smoky red wine. The bouquet is round and full, assertive, harmonious, fruity, and the taste is warm, generous, full of masculine dignity and authority. It's a wine with a lot of dimension, a lot to think about, and a lot to enjoy. I hope you agree when you try it. Price range: 24 oz, $2.59–2.89.

ΨΨΨΨ UVITA BURGUNDY   Produced & bottled by Dobboletta y Cia., Mendoza, Argentina. Rating: 12. Distribution: C. Welcome to a pleasant foreign experience! This low-cost import has a lovely forthright nose, filled with fruit and tinged with spice. It's refined and rounded, as is the taste, full of fruit and flowers and herbs and sunshine. It's a healthy, outdoorsy wine, redolent of wood nymphs, tree sprites, and a rich harvest. A *foreign* harvest. Try it. Price range: 24 oz, $.99–1.39.

Ψ VERDILLAC BORDEAUX SUPERIEUR   Bottled by Maison A. Roux, Bordeaux, France. Rating: 8. Distribution: C. This light-colored wine has a shy nose, void of defect, and a light, thin, somewhat astringent taste. It's pleasantly dry, has quality overtones, and I have an idea that it might improve in the bottle if you can wait a few years. My problem is, I can never wait! Price range: 24 oz, $2.98–3.29.

♀♀ VILLA BANFI ROMAN RED Bottled by C.A.C.S. Ariccia, Rome, Italy. Rating: 9. Distribution: B. This wine has an outdoorsy attractiveness that makes no demands on the intellect. The nose is simple and acceptable, and there's even a hint of spice, if you strain for it. In the mouth it's soft, light, semidry, and nicely filled with fruit. It's just tart enough to be nicely refreshing and energetic, and I think you may like it. Price range: 24 oz, $1.99–2.49.

♀ VILLA MARIA BARDOLINO Bottled by CA. VI. SA., Verona, Italy. Rating: 8+. Distribution: B. This orangy-red wine has a light, pleasant nose that is pretty bashful, but contains no wrong notes. The taste is satisfying without being extraordinary in any way. The wine is dry, light in body, nicely balanced, and very enjoyable though not very consequential. Price range: 50 oz, $3.49–3.99.

♀♀♀ VILLA MARIA VALPOLICELLA Bottled by CA. VI. SA., Verona, Italy. Rating: 10. Distribution: B. This is a light, dry, spirited wine that offers a lot of pleasure without demanding a lot of thought. The nose is clean, rounded, uncomplicated without being simple-minded. It's nice to sniff at. The fruit is quiet, but it's there. The taste is lively and fruity, like the nose, and the overall sensation is one of relaxation and geniality. Price range: 50 oz, $3.49–3.99.

♀♀ VIÑA SAN PEDRO GATO NEGRO Produced & bottled by Wagner, Stein y Cia., Chile. Rating: 9+. Distribution: C. The color of this Chilean import is a rich, purply red. The nose is aggressive, and there's a slightly weedy vigor to it that is more athletic than aristocratic, but it's engaging and decent enough. In the mouth it's genial and refreshing, walking the line between sweet and dry, and the effect is of cleanliness and refreshment, without sophistication. It's a nice change of pace. Price range: 23.3 oz, $1.49–1.69.

VIÑA UNDURRAGA PINOT   Produced & bottled by Viña Undurraga, Estación Sta. Ana, Chile. Rating: 7. Distribution: C. Unfortunately, this interesting-looking wine needs more redeeming features to be worth a try. It's a deep garnet color, but the nose has a rather disagreeable component that is echoed in its astringent flavor. Too bad. Price range: 24 oz, $.99–1.09.

♀♀ WEIBEL CALIFORNIA CLASSIC BURGUNDY   Produced & bottled by Weibel Champagne Vineyards, Mission San Jose, California. Rating: 9. Distribution: C. This wine is a transparent scarlet color, with a slightly aggressive nose that only occasionally seems raw. However, since there's fruit and zestiness in it, too, that doesn't really matter. The wine is moderately dry in the mouth, crisp and athletic, and what with the generous measure of fruit it offers, you'll probably like it as much as I do. Price range: 25.6 oz, $1.99–2.39.

WENTE BROTHERS ZINFANDEL   Produced & bottled by Wente Brothers, Livermore, California. Rating: 7+. Distribution: B. Wente's Zinfandel has a ponderous, dank aroma that displays little charm. There's lots of fruit in the mouth, however, but it's a touch on the sweet side, and in general the wine is acceptable but undistinguished. Price range: 25.6 oz, $2.75–3.29.

♉♉♉ WINEMASTERS CALIFORNIA CABERNET SAUVIGN-
ON   Made & bottled by Winemasters' Guild, San Francisco, California. Rating: 10. Distribution: A. This
wine has a rich, raspberry color, and a soft, rounded,
modestly fruited nose. The aroma is quiet, demure,
pleasing, and the taste is dry, with a moderately light
body and a supple, woodsy flavor. There's fruit and
there's charm, and the picture that comes to my mind
is that of a handsome, slender denizen of the forest
slipping quietly and gracefully through the trees. If
that's too poetic, I guess you'll have to try it, and paint
your own picture. Price range: 25.6 oz, $2.49–2.99.

♉♉ WINEMASTERS CALIFORNIA MOUNTAIN BURGUN-
DY Made & bottled by Winemasters' Guild, San
Francisco, California. Rating: 9+. Distribution: A.
This Burgundy is a clear, clean scarlet with purple
tones. The nose is fresh, ingenuous, simple, fruity.
The taste is pleasantly full, rounded, supple, semidry,
and very drinkable. There's lots of fruit and a nice acid
balance, and if you're looking for a nice, simple,
enjoyable wine at a good price, this may be it. Price
range: 25.6 oz, $1.69–1.99.

WINEMASTERS CALIFORNIA RUBY CABERNET Made &
bottled by The Winemasters' Guild, San Francisco,
California. Rating: 5+. Distribution: A. Color: on the
dark side. Nose: feeble, stale, little to offer. Taste:
common, stale, baked, thin, negative backtaste. Recommendation: Figure it out for yourself. Price range:
25.4 oz, $1.89–2.19.

♉♉ WINEMASTERS CALIFORNIA ZINFANDEL Made & bottled by Winemasters' Guild, San Francisco, Califor-

nia. Rating: 9+. Distribution: A. The color is a rich, dark, ecclesiastical scarlet. The nose is clean, uncomplicated, honest, fruity. The taste is healthy and robust, full of fruits, berries, and the simple, sunshiny outdoors. Don't look for complexity, it isn't there. But what is there is plenty for lots of occasions. Price range: 25.6 oz, $1.89–2.19.

8

White Wines

♀♀♀ ADRIATICA RIZLING FROM FRUSKA GORA   Produced & bottled by Adriatica, Yugoslavia. Rating: 10. Distribution: B. This handsome green-gold wine has a subtle, attractive, fruity nose, but it's the taste that shows off its best points. This is full, rounded, pleasingly sweet in a sort of smooth, honeyed way, and the overall sensation is that of a lovely, feminine, mature white wine. Price range: 24 oz, $2.39–2.69.

AKADAMA LIGHT WHITE   Produced & bottled by Suntory, Ltd., Tokyo & Osaka, Japan. Rating: 6. Distribution: A. This is a sweet, syrupy wine with a burnt-caramel flavor. Sweet-wine lovers may pardon the baked flavor and the hot-weather nose, especially since the wine is such a beautiful color in the glass—deep, rich, and tawny. The rest of us, I expect, will prefer to pass it by in favor of something else. Price range: 25.4 oz, $1.59–1.99.

ALMADÉN CALIFORNIA CHABLIS   Made & bottled by Almadén Vineyards, Los Gatos, California. Rating: 7. Distribution: A. The aroma of this Chablis is austere, which is obviously okay, and a little dank, which isn't. In the mouth there's the same dry austerity, which is fine for a Chablis, but there's an unfortunate bitter tone and a degree of flatness that keeps this wine from getting out of the middle ranges of acceptability. Price range: 25.6 oz, $1.99–2.25.

♀♀ ALMADÉN CALIFORNIA FRENCH COLOMBARD   Made & bottled by Almadén Vineyards, Los Gatos, California. Rating: 9. Distribution: A. The nose is very pleasant, despite a slight touch of sharpness, not enough to cause you any problem. The taste gives a rounded, uncomplicated picture of the fruit that went into its making. It's a pleasant, inviting wine with a clear, golden color, and you should give it a try. Price range: 25.6 oz, $1.99–2.25.

♀ ALMADÉN CALIFORNIA MOUNTAIN RHINE   Made & bottled by Almadén Vineyards, Los Gatos, California. Rating: 8+. Distribution: A. I got a smell of apples in the clean, light aroma of this wine, and I got a taste of the same apples, fairly well diluted, in the taste. It was a nice smell and taste, and I found it appealing. The wine is tipped toward the sweet end of things, and it could be that you'd find it intriguing. Nothing like trying a bottle to find out. Price range: 25.6 oz, $1.79–2.10.

ALMADÉN CALIFORNIA MOUNTAIN WHITE CHABLIS   Made & bottled by Almadén Vineyards, Los Gatos, California. Rating: 7. Distribution: A. This is a dry, thin wine in which the fruit seems to hold back both in the nose and the mouth. The color is pale and clear, the nose acceptable but dour. The wine itself seems lacking in generosity, unwilling to give. Alas! Price range: 25.6 oz, $1.79–2.10.

ALMADÉN CALIFORNIA MOUNTAIN WHITE SAUTERNE Made & bottled by Almadén Vineyards, Los Gatos, California. Rating: 6+. Distribution: A. This wine is almost pale enough to be mistaken for water. There isn't much of an aroma, but what there is is acceptable enough, even though the message is little more than "It's wine, all right." In the mouth the wine is thin, sourish, and astringent. Price range: 25.6 oz, $1.79–2.10.

ARAL SUNGURLU Produced & bottled by Zeki Aral, Ankara, Turkey. Rating: 7+. Distribution: C. A wine from Turkey has to be interesting. This one is. It has a medium sherry color, an innocuous nose with just a touch of hot weather in it, and a sweetish, slightly heavy, slightly baked flavor. It's well balanced, and despite a modest bitter tone, it's pleasant enough. So, if you're adventuresome, try it. If you're not, read on. Price range: 24 oz, $1.59–1.99.

♀♀♀ B & G PONTET-LATOUR Bottled by Barton & Guestier, Blanquefort, Gironde, France. Rating: 11. Distribution: A. There is a faint greenish cast to this pale, clear wine. The nose is hard, austere, without flowers or any indication of fun and games. This is a serious, very dry wine, and it stands on its dignity and breeding. It has style rather than charm, and would crackle nicely with the fish course. But remember, it's no kindergarten wine, no dancing around the May-pole! It's authentic and formal, and all in all, quite a good dry white wine. Price range: 24 oz, $2.99–3.19.

BARENGO CELLARS CALIFORNIA CHABLIS   Produced & bottled by Barengo Vineyards, Acampo, California. Rating: 7. Distribution: B. This Chablis has a pale, bleached look, and an unappealing, somewhat metal-lic nose. The flavor is modestly sweet, unspectacular, and although it may help you wash down some lunch or dinner, completely forgettable. Price range: 25.6 oz, $1.99–2.19.

♀♀♀♀ BEAMEISTER LIEBFRAUMILCH   Produced & bottled by GG. Balthasar Diedert, Munster-Sarmsheim, Ger-many. Rating: 11+. Distribution: B. There is a deli-cate, fresh, outdoorsy bouquet to this green-tinted golden wine. It's clean, clear, and inviting, and leads you on to its pleasing, congenial flavor. It's a taste of mature outdoor pleasures, something slightly more advanced than footraces without being any less charming and outgoing. It's well balanced, fruity, on the sweet side, and very satisfying. Try it. Price range: 23 oz, $2.99–3.19.

♀♀♀ BEAMEISTER MAY WINE   Produced & bottled by GG. Balthasar Diedert, Munster-Sarmsheim, Germa-ny. Rating: 10+. Distribution: B. A May wine, for those who've never tried one, is generally a Rhine wine that has been flavored with an herb called woodruff. It has a slightly unusual aroma and taste, and it may be the first of the "pop wines." Anyhow, it's fun to drink now and then, and when you decide to try it, this one is a very good candidate. It's a transparent lemony gold, and with its woodruff it smells to me of cinnamon, a touch of clove, some nutmeg, and some tree moss. The taste is pleasing, slightly mysterious, and should bring on visions of elves and other woodland sprites darting in and out of trees. Give it a try—you could like it a lot! Price range: 23 oz, $2.99–3.19.

ΨΨΨΨΨ BEAMEISTER MOSELBLUEMCHEN Produced & bottled by GG. Balthasar Diedert, Munster-Sarmsheim, Germany. Rating: 13. Distribution: B. A nice, nice wine, light in color, with flashes of green. The nose is inviting and invigorating, fresh and full of fruit. The taste has gentle sweetness, fruit, charm, acid to compensate the moderate sweetness, and I think you'll be glad you bought a bottle. Price range: 23 oz, $2.99–3.19.

ΨΨΨ BEAULIEU VINEYARD NAPA VALLEY CHABLIS Produced & bottled by Beaulieu Vineyard, Rutherford, California. Rating: 10+. Distribution: B. In color and nose Beaulieu's Chablis starts out very much like a French Chablis. The color is pale and strawlike, and the nose has the assertiveness and masculine hardness of a "real" Chablis. In the mouth, however, the similarity disappears, and the wine comes back to California with touches of sweetness and fruit, and none of the flintiness you'd associate with its French cousin. You'll like it—at least, I did, and gave it a very good mark. Price range: 25.6 oz, $2.99–3.19.

ΨΨΨΨ BERINGER CALIFORNIA TRAUBENGOLD Cellared & bottled by Beringer Vineyards, St. Helena, California. Rating: 11+. Distribution: A. This pale golden wine has a piquant bouquet, crisp and clean and fruity and fresh, and it foretells the attractive taste. There's fruit aplenty in the taste, and an engaging natural sweetness. The acid is moderate, but still very satisfactory, and as I taste this wine I see men in whites and women with parasols playing croquet in the sunshine on an enormous lawn. Try it—see what *you* see! Price range: 25.6 oz, $2.75–2.99.

ȣȣ BERINGER NORTH COAST CHABLIS   Produced & bottled by Beringer Vineyards, St. Helena, California. Rating: 9+. Distribution: A. There's a hint of licorice and vanilla extract in the aroma of this pleasant, straw-colored wine, and the flavor is unusual, too: lemony, light, refreshing, and altogether very enjoyable. A good value. Price range: 25.6 oz, $2.15–2.49.

ȣȣȣȣ BERINGER NORTH COAST CHENIN BLANC   Produced & bottled by Beringer Vineyards, St. Helena, California. Rating: 11+. Distribution: A. This Chenin Blanc has a pale barley color and a light, clean nose full of fresh fruit. In the mouth you'll find a smooth, honeyed flavor, fairly well on the sweet side, offering agreeable fruit sensations and a good balance. You won't serve it with the fish, because of the sweetness, but it could be very nice as an apéritif, or with a sweet dessert. Price range: 25.6 oz, $2.75–2.99.

ȣȣ BERINGER NORTH COAST GREY RIESLING   Produced & bottled by Beringer Vineyards, St. Helena, California. Rating: 9. Distribution: A. The nose has no great message for us, other than that of modesty and cleanliness. The taste is moderately dry, pleasingly youthful, fresh, and endowed with good quantities of fruit and sunshine. The color is a pale amber, with a slightly tawny cast. A pleasing wine. Price range: 25.6 oz, $2.75–2.99.

♀♀♀♀♀ BLUE MAX LIEBFRAUMILCH   Bottled & shipped by Van Hooff & Co., St. Aldegund/Mosel, Germany. Rating: 13+. Distribution: B. This wine has a lovely inner spirit. I know that sounds like winesmanship talk, but it is really a delightful wine. The color is light and clear, the nose is full of fruit and flowers. The taste is naturally sweet, warm, and genial, bursting with health and a vigorous maturity, and as I drink it, I seem to see maidens dancing on grassy hillsides in colorful native costumes. If it can do that for me, think what it can do for you! Price range: 23.7 oz, $2.99–3.19.

♀♀♀♀ BLUE MAX NIERSTEINER GUTES DOMTAL   Produced & bottled by Van Hooff & Co., St. Aldegund/Mosel, Germany. Rating: 12. Distribution: B. This Niersteiner is full of flowers, fruit, and sunshine, both in the nose and the mouth. It's lovely, sweet, well made, and possessed of a kind of elegant innocence that I think you will enjoy. Any flaxen-haired girls who didn't turn out for the dance of the Liebfraumilch are sure to turn up for the Niersteiner, along with any number of congenial young men in lederhosen. Price range: 23.7 oz, $2.99–3.19.

BOORDY VINEYARDS BOORDYBLÜMCHEN   Produced & bottled by Boordy Vineyards, Westfield, New York. Rating: 6. Distribution: C. There is obviously some thought and care that has gone into the making of this deep lemony golden wine, but it doesn't come off.

The nose is austere and hard, and over it all is a sensation of wet, moldy hay. In the mouth it's dry, faintly bitter, and something less than charming. Price range: 25.6 oz, $2.19–2.49.

BOORDY VINEYARDS PINARD BLANC   Produced & bottled by Boordy Vineyards, Penn Yan, New York. Rating: 4+. Distribution: C. This wine needs to open the window and let the fresh air in. Despite its rich, sunny color, there's no sunshine in the bouquet or in the taste. The nose is closed in and makes me think remotely of the smell of silos in my childhood. The taste is moldy and charmless, and my advice is to forget it. Price range: 25.6 oz, $1.89–2.39.

BOORDY VINEYARDS WHITE WINE   Produced & bottled by Boordy Vineyards, Penn Yan, New York. Rating: 7. Distribution: C. Boordy's white is an unremarkable wine, one of those not bad/not good wines that seem to make up a lot of what gets into bottles these days. It has a dry sherry color, a very ordinary, slightly dank nose, and a dryish, decent, undistinguished taste. Price range: 25.6 oz, $1.89–2.39.

♀♀ BRONCO CALIFORNIA CHABLIS   Cellared & bottled by JFJ Bronco Winery, Ceres, California. Rating: 9. Distribution: C. The color is wan and pale. The nose is clean, healthy, feminine, and I get a faint sensation of peaches and vanilla extract. The taste is simple and uncomplicated, lightly sweet with moderate fruitiness, and if the batch you get is the same as the batch I got, it's a great buy. Price range: 32 oz, $.99–1.19.

♀♀♀ BUENA VISTA SONOMA CHABLIS   Produced & bottled by Buena Vista Winery, Sonoma, California. Rating: 10. Distribution: B. This Chablis has a pale, wheat color and a hard, masculine nose. There's a clean, flinty austerity about it that's very classic and authentic. The taste is fruity, semidry, and somewhat steely. It's a thought-provoking wine, a wine with a fair degree of both severity and style. There's no kidding around with this wine—it's strictly for adults! Price range: 25.6 oz, $2.50–3.19.

CC VINEYARDS CALIFORNIA CHABLIS Cellared & bottled by CC Vineyard Winery, Ceres, California. Rating: 7+. Distribution: C. This is a pale, wan wine with a thin, pungent, somewhat masculine nose, lacking in fruit. The taste isn't bad; neither will it make your pulses race. It's subdued, acceptable, slightly cooked, somber, and has a general overall feeling of being unexciting and middle aged. Price range: 128 oz, $2.19–2.49.

CAMBIASO CALIFORNIA CHABLIS Made & bottled by Cambiaso Winery & Vineyards, Healdsburg, California. Rating: 6+. Distribution: C. The color is a very handsome gold. The aroma is thin and reedy, as though the fruit never ripened. My mouth's reactions on two separate occasions were: (1) yes, it's wine; (2) it's thin, deficient in fruit; (3) it's very, very ordinary; (4) it makes me think of creme soda. Creme-soda lovers may address their protests to me, in writing, please. Price range: 25.6 oz, $1.59–1.79.

🍷🍷 CARLO ROSSI'S RED MOUNTAIN CALIFORNIA CHABLIS Made & bottled by Carlo Rossi Vineyards, Modesto, California. Rating: 9. Distribution: A. This Chablis is so pale and silvery it's almost colorless. The nose is brisk, fresh, and fruity, almost saucy. The taste is light, fresh, semidry, simple, clean, light hearted. And the price is terrific! Price range: 25.4 oz, $.99–1.25.

CARLO ROSSI'S RED MOUNTAIN CALIFORNIA RHINE Made & bottled by Carlo Rossi Vineyards, Modesto, California. Rating: 7+. Distribution: A. Ordinary, run-of-the-mill, but no glaring defects. Just dull. The color is a medium honey tone, the nose has little to offer other than a faint recollection of a dank cellar. The taste is sweetish, with not much life. Price range: 25.4 oz, $.99–1.25.

CARMEL CHÂTEAU RICHON VIN BLANC D'ISRAEL Produced & bottled by Carmel Wine Growers Cooperative, Richon Le Zion, Zichron Jacob, Israel. Rating: 7. Distribution: A. This is a sweet, heavy wine with overtones of brier bushes and a few roadside weeds. It has an oldish, closed-in aroma, and an aftertaste that reminds you of the oldish, closed-in aroma. It's not awful, it's just middle of the road, and you can do better than that. Price range: 25.6 oz, $2.05–2.49.

♀ CARMEL HOCK Produced & bottled by Carmel Wine Growers Cooperative, Richon le Zion, Zichron Jacob, Israel. Rating: 8. Distribution: A. This is a good, sturdy, peasant white wine. It's vigorous, semidry, but with some pleasing natural sugar. The color is light, the wine is clean, the nose is bland. It's a case of a wine that has character without having great beauty, and while you won't exclaim over it, you'll know you're enjoying a sound, well-made wine. Price range: 25.6 oz, $2.05–2.49.

CASTILLO ARDAU BLANCO ESPECIAL Bottled by Ardau, S.A., Areta-Llodio, Spain. Rating: 7+. Distribution:

C. For a white table wine, this one is on the dark side, the color of a medium sherry. The aroma is shy, decent, and unremarkable, and the wine itself is heavy, almost syrupy. With a little more acid and slightly better finish, it could score extra points as a sort of specialty table wine, maybe something to go with a dessert. As it is, it's still interesting and worth a try when you're looking for something different. Price range: 24 oz, $1.39–1.79.

CHÂTEAU VIN CALIFORNIA CHABLIS   Produced by Lodi Vintners, Bottled by Carnot Vintners, Acampo, California. Rating: 6+. Distribution: C. You can't really say anything terrible about this Chablis, but you can't say anything nice, either. It's a watery, common, characterless white wine, with a slightly aggressive, but terribly ordinary nose. Well-chilled, it will wash down a meal, and that's about the size of it. Price range: 25.6 oz, $.99–1.19.

CHÂTEAU VIN CALIFORNIA FRENCH COLOMBARD   Bottled by Carnot Vintners, Acampo, California. Rating: 7. Distribution: C. Here we are in the middle of the road again. An unremarkable wine with an unremarkable nose and a simple, unremarkable taste. It's not bad at its price, but I doubt that you want to settle for that. Anyhow, it has some sweetness, a touch of bitterness in the aftertaste, and it's drinkable, but not much more. Price range: 25.6 oz, $1.49–1.69.

ΨΨΨΨ CHRISTIAN BROTHERS CHATEAU LA SALLE   Produced & bottled by The Christian Brothers, Napa, California. Rating: 12. Distribution: A. Of its kind, and I have to say that again, *of its kind* it is a terrific wine. The kind? Well, it's something like the sweet sauternes of France. It has a handsome amber color and a truly lovely nose, inviting, fragrant, warm, fruity, and wholesome. In the mouth it's definitely sweet and fruity, not the kind of white wine you'd serve with a fish course, but it would be a sensation served with your cherries jubilee! Price range: 25.4 oz, $2.35–2.55.

ΨΨΨΨ CHRISTIAN BROTHERS SELECT CALIFORNIA CHABLIS Produced & bottled by The Christian Brothers, Napa, California. Rating: 11+. Distribution: A. Finding a decent white wine at a reasonable price always seems harder than finding a decent red. Fortunately, the Christian Brothers have come to the rescue with this Chablis. It has a rich, lemony color and a generous nose, fruity and interesting. In the mouth it's smooth, fresh, with a good acid balance and only a touch of sweetness. Hurrah for the Brotherhood! Price range: 25.4 oz, $2.15–2.39.

Ψ CHRISTIAN BROTHERS SELECT CALIFORNIA HAUT SAUTERNE Produced & bottled by The Christian Brothers, Napa, California. Rating: 8+. Distribution: A. Color: deep lemony gold. Nose: so-so, pungent, slightly baked, acceptable. Taste: sweetish, a little syrupy, full of sweet, ripe grapes, delightful for sweet-wine lovers. Is there a slight background taste you wish weren't there? Yes, there is. But for the sweet-wine people, it's still a nice wine. Price range: 25.4 oz, $2.15–2.39.

ΨΨΨΨΨ CHRISTIAN BROTHERS SELECT CALIFORNIA SAUTERNE Produced & bottled by The Christian Brothers, Napa, California. Rating: 13. Distribution: A.

This one is a goodie. I have to warn you that it has a moderate sweetness, so if you only cotton to dry, dry wines, you won't understand why I think this one is so good. It's a lemony gold color, and the nose is velvety, aromatic, fruity, and ingenuous. In the mouth the wine is clean, full, round, with moderate acid, and shows lots of sunshine and lovely grapes. I think it's a winner. And I think it's worth your time and money to see if I'm right. Price range: 25.4 oz, $2.15–2.39.

♀♀♀ CRESTA BLANCA CALIFORNIA BLANC DE BLANC Made & bottled by Cresta Blanca Winery, San Francisco, California. Rating: 10. Distribution: B. This honey-colored wine has a deep, clear, rounded bouquet, delicate and mature. The taste is soft and supple, on the sweet side, but compensated with a moderate amount of acid. It's a charming, feminine wine, and well worth your trying a bottle. Price range: 25.6 oz, $1.99–2.39.

♀♀ CRESTA BLANCA CALIFORNIA CHENIN BLANC Made & bottled by Cresta Blanca Winery, San Francisco, California. Rating: 9. Distribution: B. I guess it's possible to be charming and sedate at the same time, because that's what this wine is. The color is light and clean, the nose is shy but attractive, the taste has plenty of fruit which comes through in a lightly sweet way, and makes me think not of youth, but of maturity, sort of a settled but optimistic and attractive middle age. Price range: 25.6 oz, $2.50–2.79.

♀♀♀ CRESTA BLANCA CALIFORNIA FRENCH COLOMBARD Made & bottled by Cresta Blanca Winery, San Francisco, California. Rating: 10. Distribution: B. The color is pale and tawny, and the nose is clean, quiet, acceptable, without making any great statements about fruit, flowers, or other subjects. The taste is elegant. It has a pleasing fruit sweetness with a moderate sweet-sour counterpoint, and it's a gentle wine, not a vigorous one, lovely and mature and elegant. Price range: 25.6 oz, $1.99–2.39.

CRESTA BLANCA CALIFORNIA MOUNTAIN CHABLIS   Made & bottled by Cresta Blanca Winery, San Francisco, California. Rating: 7+. Distribution: B. This Chablis is lively, brash, and assertive, but just a little bit too goaty and green for my taste. Yes, it's quite drinkable, and yes, someone else might like it quite a bit, but it's just too bumptious and aggressive to suit me. Price range: 25.4 oz, $1.99–2.39.

♀ FAMIGLIA CRIBARI CALIFORNIA MOUNTAIN CHABLIS   Made & bottled by B. Cribari & Sons, San Francisco, California. Rating: 8+. Distribution: A. This is a very pale, silvery, almost colorless wine with a very serious approach to life. The nose is a bit severe, maybe even stuffy, and the taste is adult, formal, almost dour. This may make the wine sound uninviting, but actually in many ways it's more like a real French Chablis than many California wines that carry that name. So, if your taste runs toward restraint, and you want to try a semidry wine built along those lines, try this one. Price range: 25.4 oz, $1.29–1.49.

FAMIGLIA CRIBARI CALIFORNIA SAUTERNE   Made & bottled by B. Cribari & Sons, San Francisco, California. Rating: 7+. Distribution: A. This clean-looking pale wine has a brisk, young, greenish nose and a taste that's quite decent, but a bit common. The wine is simple and refreshing, semidry, equipped with adequate fruit, and I don't want to say anything against it. It's a nice, middling wine, not at all hard to enjoy under the right circumstances of food and companionship. Price range: 25.4 oz, $1.29–1.49.

FAMIGLIA CRIBARI CALIFORNIA VINO BIANCO DA PRANZO Made & bottled by B. Cribari & Sons, San Francisco, California. Rating: 7+. Distribution: A. The color is a bit wan, the nose is clean, ordinary, nothing special. In the mouth it's sweetish, and shows some agreeable fruit. On balance, it's ordinary, and I think you can do better despite the good price. Price range: 25.4 oz, $1.29–1.49.

DELICATO ESPECIALLY SELECTED CALIFORNIA CHABLIS BLANC Produced & bottled by Delicato Vineyards, Manteca, California. Rating: 7. Distribution: B. There is a touch of wet cellar floors in the nose of this Chablis. It's not pronounced, so the nose is tolerable, but it's there. The taste is semidry, masculine, and displays a tinge of bitterness. It has a decent balance of fruit and acid, and it's drinkable, but I think you want more than that. Price range: 25.6 oz, $1.39–1.59.

♀ DELICATO ESPECIALLY SELECTED CALIFORNIA CHENIN BLANC Produced & bottled by Delicato Vineyards, Manteca, California. Rating: 8. Distribution: B. This wine has no great defects, but neither does it have anything much to offer in a positive sense. The color is pale, the nose is modest, but there's some fruit and some nice balance going for it in the mouth. Not a bad wine at all; a sound wine, in fact. You'll probably enjoy it. Price range: 25.6 oz, $1.99–2.29.

♀ DELICATO ESPECIALLY SELECTED CALIFORNIA RHINE Produced & bottled by Delicato Vineyards, Manteca, California. Rating: 8. Distribution: B. The gift this wine has to offer is very modest, but sometimes modest gifts are okay. The color is light straw, the aroma is a bit hard to locate, but when you do, it's clean and fruity. There's not a lot of character to the taste—it's simple-minded but decent enough, which may be the definition of a *vin ordinaire*. Price range: 25.6 oz, $1.39–1.59.

ESTORIL WHITE WINE   Produced & bottled by Meireles, Baptista & Ca., Lda., Oporto, Portugal. Rating: 7+. Distribution: C. This import has a rich lemony color and a fair nose, with an unfortunate whiff of something metallic. Nonetheless, it has a decent flavor, nothing special but certainly drinkable. There is a hint of bitterness in the aftertaste, but well-chilled, it won't keep you from enjoying a pleasant dinner. In fact, it will add just a bit to it. Price range: 24 oz, $1.19–1.39.

♀ FETZER VINEYARDS MENDOCINO PREMIUM WHITE Produced & bottled by Fetzer Vineyards, Redwood Valley, California. Rating: 8+. Distribution: C. Fetzer's Premium White has a light straw color and a presentable but unspectacular nose that now and then seems to have a touch of dankness. Still, the taste is pleasant, clean, and slightly sedate, with a modest nod toward sweetness, and I think you'll enjoy it. Price range: 25.6 oz, $2.25–2.65.

♀♀ FOLONARI SOAVE   Produced & bottled by SPAL, Pastrengo (Verona), Italy. Rating: 9. Distribution: B. This wine has a somewhat formal character. The color is light and attractive, and the nose, while somewhat reluctant, shows some fruit in a rather restrained way. The taste is both amiable and thoughtful, light, halfway between sweet and dry, and with a gentle tartness. It's a wine of some quality, but it's a rather quiet, genteel kind, without any hint of flashiness or dash. Price range: 67.6 oz, $3.79–4.19.

♀♀ FONTANA CANDIDA FRASCATI SUPERIORE   Produced & bottled by Vinidi F.C.S.p.a., Monteporzio Catone, Italy. Rating: 9. Distribution: B. There is an unusual licorice flavor that turns up in this light, clear wine. There's no hint of it in the nose, which is ripe, rounded, charming, and delicately fruity. It comes through, however, in the taste, which is dry, thin, and refreshing. It's different, and it's interesting. Whether it's to your taste is up to you, of course. Price range: 24 oz, $2.99–3.19.

FOPPIANO CALIFORNIA CHABLIS   Made & bottled by Foppiano Wine Co., Healdsburg, California. Rating: 7+. Distribution: C. This tawny golden Chablis has a brash nose that comes across as green and aggressive. The taste is semidry, countrified, and a trifle coarse. It's not a bad wine, just a common one, and in spite of it all, a wine that can still help a simple meal taste a little better. Price range: 25.6 oz, $1.49–1.69.

FRANZIA CALIFORNIA CHABLIS BLANC   Made & bottled by Franzia Brothers, Ripon, California. Rating: 7.

Distribution: B. The color is bright and sunny, the rest of the experience is ordinary, uncomplicated, and, I guess, common. The nose has little to offer, the taste is decent—dry, light, unremarkable, and acceptable. Price range: 25.4 oz, $.99–1.29.

♈♈ FRATELLI CELLA BIANCO   Produced & bottled by I. W. C., Modena, Italy. Rating: 9. Distribution: B. There's a slight spritz, or carbonation, when you pour this deep, rich-looking, honey-gold wine. The nose is green and bumptious in a rude, peasant way. You'll experience more spritz when you take a mouthful, and you'll be rewarded with an unusual, heavy, voluptuous taste, slightly sweet, ripe, full of fruit, healthy, and sensual. It's an unusual wine, one you may love or hate, the kind about which you have to say that "of its type" it's very enjoyable. Price range: 24 oz, $2.29–2.89.

♈♈ GALLO CALIFORNIA CHABLIS BLANC   Made & bottled by Ernest & Julio Gallo, Modesto, California. Rating: 9. Distribution: A. There is a modest amount of fruit and flowers in the nose of this pale, tawny wine. The nose is clean and straightforward, and the taste is gentle, feminine, undemanding, nicely balanced, with some modest sweetness. I predict you'll like it. Price range: 25.4 oz, $1.39–1.79.

♈♈ GALLO CALIFORNIA CHENIN BLANC   Vinted & cellared & bottled by Ernest & Julio Gallo, Modesto, California. Rating: 9+. Distribution: A. The color is a pale gold. The nose is not terribly intrusive, but what does make it across the threshold is clean and fresh and fruity. The taste is semidry, with reminders of sweetness, crisp, fruity, and youthful. There's just enough acid to lend a little vigor and refreshment, and all in all, it's an enjoyable wine. Price range: 25.4 oz, $1.69–2.19.

♀ GALLO CALIFORNIA FRENCH COLOMBARD Vinted & cellared & bottled by Ernest & Julio Gallo, Modesto, California. Rating: 8. Distribution: A. This colombard has a rather modest nose without any particular defects, and a taste that isn't bad, but isn't wonderful, either. I think you will probably find it a suitable accompaniment to a meal somewhere along the line. It's one of those serviceable, undistinguished wines that help keep the world turning on its axis without getting anyone excessively excited. Price range: 25.4 oz, $1.49–1.89.

♀♀♀ GALLO CALIFORNIA RHINE GARTEN Made & bottled by Ernest & Julio Gallo, Modesto, California. Rating: 10. Distribution: A. There is an ample, generous feeling in this pale, clear wine, something simple but big hearted and very enjoyable. The nose is light and airy, and the ripe fruit comes through easily. The taste is on the sweet side, soft and round, with a modest, engaging acid balance. Chill it well and enjoy it! Price range: 25.4 oz, $1.29–1.69.

♀♀ GALLO CALIFORNIA RHINE WINE Made & bottled by Gallo Vineyards, Modesto, California. Rating: 9. Distribution: A. The Rhine that flows through Modesto bears no relation to Germany's Rhine, but who cares? This is an amber-colored wine with a pleasing, aromatic nose that seems to include apricots, cider, and iced tea. The taste is sweet, slightly heavy, and unusual, as though it were made from unfamiliar grapes and maybe some nectarines. Nonetheless, it's a very pleasant wine, and it's my guess that it might do very nicely with a somewhat sweet dessert. Try it and see for yourself. Price range: 25.4 oz, $1.39–1.79.

♀♀♀ GALLO CALIFORNIA RIESLING   Vinted & cellared & bottled by Ernest & Julio Gallo, Modesto, California. Rating: 10. Distribution: A. This Riesling has a modest nose, but it's a nice, fresh, pleasingly green nose, and it betokens very attractive wine. Behind the freshness there is a soft, feminine wine, more charming than stylish, full of flowers, fruit, and sunshine. It's a lazy afternoon wine, and if you like lazy afternoons as much as I do, you'll probably also like this wine. Price range: 25.4 oz, $1.69–2.19.

♀♀ GANCIA SOAVE CLASSICO SUPERIORE   Produced by Figli Gancia & Cia., Canelli, Italy. Rating: 9+. Distribution: B. This pale, greenish-gold wine has a shy, grassy, springlike aroma, and a taste to match. It's a dry, zesty, outdoorsy kind of wine, genial and somewhat unusual in its overall character of grassiness rather than fruitiness. Not for everyone, but those who like it may like it a great deal. Price range: 24 oz, $2.89–3.29.

♀♀ GINJAL WHITE WINE   Produced & bottled by So. Com. Theotonio Pereira, Lisbon, Portugal. Rating: 9. Distribution: C. This is a rather dark white wine, amber colored, more like a sherry than a white. The nose is very definite, nervy, pungent, and in its way a pleasurable sensation. In the mouth it is fresh with a pleasing tart edge, and makes me think of Chinese food: sweet and sour. It's not like a French wine, and it's not like a California wine. But it's still a nice change from your everyday fare, and you might enjoy springing it on your friends. Price range: 24 oz, $1.29–1.59.

GIUMARRA CALIFORNIA CLASSIC CHABLIS Produced & bottled by Giumarra Vineyards, Edison, California. Rating: 6+. Distribution: C. The color is deep gold. The nose is acceptable, a trifle sharp, a trifle baked. There is a slight bitterness in the sweetish taste of the wine, perhaps an echo of the hot-weather nose, and while it's drinkable, it's just not terribly inviting. Price range: 25.6 oz, $1.59–2.25.

GOLD SEAL CHARLES FOURNIER CHABLIS NATURE Produced & bottled by Gold Seal Vineyards, Hammondsport, New York. Rating: 6+. Distribution: C. The nose of this light colored, attractively named Chablis has very little to offer. It's not bad or offensive, it's just very modest, in addition to which I get a faint odor of mothballs. The taste is musty, with earthy overtones and an occasional hint of bitterness. Not too much here for you, I'm afraid. Price range: 25.6 oz, $2.35–2.65.

GRÃO VASCO DÃO Produced & shipped by Vinicola do Vale do Dão, Lda., Viseu, Portugal. Rating: 7+. Distribution: B. If a wine can be said to be homely, this is that wine. It's not ugly, just homely, and that means acceptable, serviceable, drinkable. The nose is stuffy, closed in, and the taste is dry, stuffy, and dour. Despite all this, there's moderate fruitiness and a certain amount of refreshing tartness, plus a handsome golden, medium sherry color. The overall effect, however, is still very middle-of-the-road and, well, homely. Price range: 25 oz, $1.99–2.99.

GROWERS CALIFORNIA CHABLIS Made & bottled by California Growers Winery, San Francisco, California. Rating: 7+. Distribution: A. The wine looks watery and washed out. The nose is unusual—light, clean, and with a hint of licorice. The taste is dry, thin, stingy with the goodies, and although it is a curious wine, and not a bad wine, I doubt that you'd want to make it a habit. Price range: 25.6 oz, $.88–1.09.

GROWERS CALIFORNIA CHENIN BLANC Produced & bottled by California Growers Winery, San Francisco, California. Rating: 7+. Distribution: A. This is a pale, straw-colored wine with a slightly bitter tone in its aroma. In the mouth it's light, dry, fairly ordinary, and has that same elusive trace of bitterness. Quite drinkable, but quite ordinary. Price range: 25.6 oz, $1.29–1.59.

GROWERS CALIFORNIA FRENCH COLOMBARD Produced & bottled by California Growers Winery, San Francisco, California. Rating: 7+. Distribution: A. The color is pale and watery, the nose is bashful and undistinguished, though clean. The taste is thin, characterless, on the flat side, and has some sweetness. It's not a bad wine, but the price is the best thing about it. Price range: 25.6 oz, $1.29–1.59.

GUASTI CALIFORNIA CHENIN BLANC Made & bottled by Guasti Vintners, Delano, California. Rating: 5. Distribution: B. The color is pleasant, the nose and mouth are not. The nose is baked, and conjures up recollections of burnt caramel. The taste is no better—baked and uninviting. Price range: 25.6 oz, $1.49–1.79.

♀♀♀ GUASTI CALIFORNIA FRENCH COLOMBARD Made & bottled by Guasti Vintners, Delano, California. Rating: 10+. Distribution: B. Here's a surprise for you, a low-priced Colombard that beats out a lot of its higher-priced brethren. The color is on the pale side, the aroma is charming in a modest, feminine way, supple and floral, and the taste keeps right on in the same fashion. It's delicately sweet, light, fragile, and has lots of fruit and flowers, but don't ask me to tell you the variety. I think you'll like it. Price range: 25.6 oz, $1.49–1.79.

GUILD VINO DA TAVOLA CALIFORNIA WHITE Made & bottled by Guild Wine Co., Lodi, California. Rating: 6+. Distribution: B. This wine is pale and attractive, and has a simple, slightly greenish nose without defect or complication. There's a slight mustiness to the taste that somehow gets in the way of the fruit and general refreshment, and the results will have to be labeled very ordinary. Price range: 25.4 oz, $1.19–1.55.

♀♀♀ HAVEMEYER LIEBFRAUMILCH Produced & bottled by Havemeyer Weine GmbH., Bingen, Germany. Rating: 10+. Distribution: B. There is an interesting grassy freshness in both the nose and mouth of this attractive import. The nose is clean, sprightly, outdoorsy, and the taste is soft, smooth, faintly herbal, with a very light acid balance. The wine is a light honey color, and seems somehow to be woodsy and forest-related in a very charming way. Price range: 23.5 oz, $2.90–3.15.

♉♉♉ HAVEMEYER MAY WINE Produced & bottled by Havemeyer Weine GmbH., Bingen, Germany. Rating: 10. Distribution: B. The nose is clean and subtle, with flowers and fruit, vanilla and herbs. The taste, of course, reveals the woodruff with which May wine is always flavored, and if you like a smooth, modest sweetness, with a delicate flavor of flowers, fruits, and herbs, you'll like May wines in general and this one in particular. I like it, anyhow. Price range: 23.5 oz, $2.79–2.99.

♀ HEITZ CELLAR CALIFORNIA CHABLIS Perfected & bottled by Heitz Wine Cellars, St. Helena, California. Rating: 8+. Distribution: C. The color is rich and lightly golden, and the nose is light, softly feminine, with a modest but engaging display of fruit. The taste is semidry, with fruit present but slightly held back, nicely balanced, and with an overall feeling of formality. Serve it with the fish course, and it will probably come off quite well. Price range: 25.4 oz, $2.49–2.99.

♉♉ HENRI DE VILLAMONT SPECIAL RESERVE BLANC Shipped by Henri de Villamont, Savigny-les-Beaune, France. Rating: 9+. Distribution: B. This is a fresh, semidry wine that is attractively tart and crisp, a wine with a slightly reluctant, fresh, clean nose. It's clear and good looking, a light honey color, and I think its fruit and balance and general spirit make it a candidate for your dinner table one of these days. Price range: 24 oz, $2.98–3.29.

♉♉♉ HERBSTSONNE WHITE WINE Produced & bottled by Heinrich Lorch, Bad Bergzabern, West Germany. Rating: 10. Distribution: C. There is an attractive touch of green in the sherry color of this German white. The aroma is fresh and jolly, with citrus overtones. The wine itself is also jolly in a full, ripe, round, and solid—almost stolid—way. The fruit is there, and also a touch of earthiness, and I get a picture of wealthy overweight burghers dressed in traditional costumes, dancing in the village square. I like the picture, and I like the wine. Price range: 24 oz, $1.39–1.99.

♀♀♀ L'HUITRIÈRE MUSCADET Produced & bottled by Roger Salmont, St. Hilaire-St. Florent, France. Rating: 11. Distribution: C. I must have found this outstanding wine at a closeout, because the price was so low. Anyhow, it's a clear, golden color with a crisp, flinty-fruity nose and a lean, dry, almost crackling flavor. It's aristocratic, spare, and athletic, and if you're serving oysters or crab or almost any seafood, you'll enjoy it infinitely more if you can have a bottle of this fine wine along with it. I just hope you can find a bottle! Price range: 24 oz, $1.99–2.79.

♀ INGLENOOK CALIFORNIA NAVALLE CHABLIS Produced & bottled by Inglenook Vineyards, San Francisco, California. Rating: 8. Distribution: A. This is a sunny-looking wine with a decent, clean, and somewhat unspectacular nose. It has some fruit, and there's fruit in the taste, too. The wine is slightly sweet, simple, light-hearted, and has a modest acid balance. Not the greatest Chablis you'll find, but attractive enough to enjoy. Price range: 25.4 oz, $1.99–2.29.

♀♀ INGLENOOK CALIFORNIA NAVALLE CHENIN BLANC Produced & bottled by Inglenook Vineyards, San Francisco, California. Rating: 9. Distribution: A. This dusky gold wine has some pleasing fruit in the nose, plus a few overtones of mustiness, which detract slightly. In the mouth, however, the wine is very inviting, offering an engaging fruitiness, a bit on the sweet side. I think it's a genial glass of refreshment, and you may think so, too. Price range: 25.4 oz, $1.99–2.29.

INGLENOOK CALIFORNIA NAVALLE FRENCH COLOMBARD Produced & bottled by Inglenook Vineyards, San Francisco, California. Rating: 6. Distribution: A. It may sound flip or smarty to say that a wine's aroma and taste remind you of old tire casings, but if that's the way it is, that's the way it is. Inglenook's Colombard isn't terrible but the old tire-cooker gets very much in the way and spoils everything. Price range: 25.4 oz, $1.99–2.29.

INGLENOOK CALIFORNIA NAVALLE RHINE   Produced & bottled by Inglenook Vineyards, San Francisco, California. Rating: 7+. Distribution: A. Another middle-of-the-roader. Flashy, deep gold in the glass, a little stringy and sharp in the nose, a very ordinary experience in the mouth. A little flat, a little sweet, ho-hum. Price range: 25.4 oz, $1.99–2.29.

♀♀♀ INGLENOOK NORTH COAST COUNTIES VINTAGE CHABLIS   Produced & bottled by Inglenook Vineyards, Rutherford, California. Rating: 10+. Distribution: A. This light, tawny Chablis has a charming, feminine nose, clean, inviting, full of fruit and flowers. The taste is dry with sweet touches, light, well balanced, and refreshing. In a way it's an ingenuous wine, but its simplicity is one of its charms. Price range: 25.4 oz., $2.50–2.89.

ITALIAN SWISS COLONY CALIFORNIA CHABLIS Produced & bottled by Italian Swiss Colony, Asti, California. Rating: 7+. Distribution: A. The nose is obtrusive, light, and fruity, the wine itself a light tawny color. The taste is semidry, with some fruit but with no special qualities. It's a very drinkable wine, but lacks the refinement that might make it score higher. Price range: 25.6 oz, $1.39–1.69.

♀♀ ITALIAN SWISS COLONY CALIFORNIA CHENIN BLANC Vinted & bottled by Italian Swiss Colony, Asti, California. Rating: 9. Distribution: A. Slightly unusual, but engaging and interesting. The color is a deep, lemony gold, and the nose is aromatic, with overtones of hard-to-place spices. It has a fruity taste with some sweetness, fairly well balanced, with those same interesting spicy overtones. You may like it, you may not like it, but you won't know if you don't try. Price range: 25.6 oz, $1.49–1.79.

♀♀ ITALIAN SWISS COLONY CALIFORNIA FRENCH COLOMBARD Vinted & bottled by Italian Swiss Colony, Asti, California. Rating: 9+. Distribution: A. There's a lovely greenish cast to this wine, and the nose shows a fruity, fresh greenness. It's a little harsh, but the taste—nicely fresh, young, jovial, pleasingly tart—makes up for it. I don't know why it makes me think of satyrs roaming the woods looking for innocent young maidens, but it's that kind of wine. If you're a satyr—or an innocent maiden—it might be worth a try. Price range: 25.6 oz, $1.49–1.79.

ITALIAN SWISS COLONY CALIFORNIA RHINE Produced & bottled by Italian Swiss Colony, Asti, California. Rating: 7+. Distribution: A. The only real problem is you have to hunt so hard to find any nose. The taste is genial enough, a little flat, but with some inviting fruit overtones. There's not a whole lot to say in favor of this wine, but there's nothing much to say against it, either, which is why it's just a trace better than average. Price range: 25.6 oz, $1.49–1.79.

♀♀ ITALIAN SWISS COLONY CALIFORNIA SAUTERNE Produced & bottled by Italian Swiss Colony, Asti, California. Rating: 9+. Distribution: A. The nose of this dry-sherry-colored Sauterne is fresh, green-apple green, almost a little raw. The taste is sprightly, fruity, sunshiny, with moderate sweetness, and if it's not velvet it's at least velveteen. And worth a try. Price range: 25.6 oz, $1.39–1.69.

ITALIAN SWISS COLONY EMERALD CHABLIS Produced & bottled by Italian Swiss Colony, Asti, California. Rating: 6+. Distribution: A. This light, lemon-colored wine has a hard, earthy nose and a syrupy taste, with overtones of something in both nose and mouth that is not totally agreeable. Since I am fond of Swiss Colony's Gold Chablis, I had hoped to find a sibling product that would provide equally good value. Alas, I'm afraid this isn't it. Price range: 25.6 oz, $1.39–1.69.

♀♀♀ ITALIAN SWISS COLONY GOLD CHABLIS Produced & bottled by Italian Swiss Colony, Asti, California. Rating: 11. Distribution: A. This wine is a crowd pleaser and a real bargain. It's a handsome, sunshiny wine with gold and green glints, and the nose is delicate, light, feminine, attractively fruity, and very fresh. The taste is fruity in the extreme, gently sweet, rounded and youthful, with a pleasingly honeyed flavor. There's even a hint of carbonation, and it's my guess that you're going to like this wine a lot. Price range: 25.6 oz, $1.39–1.69.

♀♀ KORBEL CALIFORNIA CHABLIS Made & bottled by F. Korbel & Bros., Guerneville, California. Rating: 9+. Distribution: B. There is a faint greenish cast to this attractive pale white wine. The nose is clean and fresh, and makes me think of the bloom on peaches. As a wine it's moderately dry, light, cheerful, ingenuous, and has more congeniality than style. You may enjoy it quite a bit. Price range: 25.4 oz, $2.25–2.65.

♀♀ KORBEL CALIFORNIA CHENIN BLANC Produced & bottled by F. Korbel & Bros., Guerneville, California. Rating: 9. Distribution: B. Korbel's Chenin Blanc is a quiet, attractive wine with no defects. It's light in color, with tawny tones, and the nose, while timid, is agreeable. In the mouth it's a cheerful, simple experience. The wine is on the dry side of the Chenin Blanc variety, and is pleasingly energetic and clean. Not a world champion, but a very nice wine all the same. Price range: 25.4 oz, $2.50–2.79.

KORBEL CALIFORNIA GREY RIESLING Produced & bottled by F. Korbel & Bros., Guerneville, California. Rating: 5. Distribution: B. The wine is good looking enough, but that's pretty much the size of it. The aroma is heavy and not very attractive, and I smelled burnt caramel and medicinal herbs in it. The taste was woody, bitter, and there was a slightly spoiled air about the whole thing. So it goes. Price range: 25.4 oz, $2.75–3.19.

♀♀ CHARLES KRUG NAPA VALLEY CHABLIS   Produced & bottled by Charles Krug Winery, St. Helena, California. Rating: 9+. Distribution: B. Krug's Chablis has a pale honey color and a nose that belies its very cheerful flavor. That is to say, the aroma seems a bit heavy for a wine that has the good fruit and balance that this wine has. It's a good wine and a sound wine, and I think you'll like it a good deal. Give it a try. Price range: 25.4 oz, $2.25–2.65.

♀♀♀ CHARLES KRUG NAPA VALLEY CHENIN BLANC Produced by Charles Krug Winery, St. Helena, California. Rating: 10+. Distribution: B. The color is lovely, clean and light with olive hints. The nose is modest, contains some fruit, and is quiet and clean. It's in the mouth that the wine's quality comes through. It's light, dryish, vivacious, with good balance, and with ripe, delicious fruit. It's a much better than average wine. Try it! Price range: 25.4 oz, $2.75–3.19.

CHARLES KRUG NAPA VALLEY DRY SAUTERNE   Produced & bottled by Charles Krug Winery, St. Helena, California. Rating: 7+. Distribution: B. The color is clear and slightly tawny. The nose is somber, oldish, middle of the road, acceptable. The taste is also down the middle. There's some fruit, it's not bad, it's not especially good, and the whole thing is somewhat unresolved. Price range: 25.4 oz, $2.25–2.65.

♀♀♀ CHARLES KRUG NAPA VALLEY GREY RIESLING Produced & bottled by Charles Krug Winery, St. Helena, California. Rating: 10+. Distribution: B. This is a quite attractive wine with a clean, glistening look in the glass and a fine performance in the mouth. The nose is modest but very honest and well scrubbed. It's a feminine wine, rounded, clean, with some sweetness, and I think you'll be glad you chilled a fifth of it and drew the cork just before dinner. Price range: 25.4 oz, $2.75–3.19.

ΨΨΨ CHARLES KRUG NAPA VALLEY TRAMINER Produced & bottled by Charles Krug Winery, St. Helena, California. Rating: 10+. Distribution: B. There is a dignity and force to this wine that makes it very attractive indeed. The nose has a certain austerity that admits of fruit, but seems also to offer touches of vanilla extract. The taste is crisp, dry, with traces of herb, brier, and tweed, and the total effect is one of outdoorsiness and masculinity. Price range: 25.4 oz, $2.75–3.19.

LA MANCHA SPANISH POUILLY-FUISSÉ Bottled by Torres de la Rivera, Valencia, Spain. Rating: 2. Distribution: X. Dark, orange-brown, cloudy, heavy, baked nose. Oxidized, spoiled flavor. Sad. Price range: 24 oz, $1.19–1.59.

M. LAMONT CALIFORNIA CHABLIS Produced & bottled by M. LaMont Vineyards, LaMont, California. Rating: 7. Distribution: B. There is a greenish cast to the clear, handsome color. The nose is decent and unremarkable. The taste is ordinary, simple, passable. You'll say, "Yes, it's wine; yes, it's white; yes, I'll have some more," but you won't remember what you drank. Price range: 25.4 oz, $1.69–1.99.

M. LAMONT CALIFORNIA FRENCH COLOMBARD Produced & bottled by M. LaMont Vineyards, LaMont, California. Rating: 5+. Distribution: B. M. LaMont's Colom-

bard appears to have been made in Akron, Ohio.
There is a rubbery, cooked character that pervades
both the aroma and the taste, and it is hardly the kind
of thing that will make you want to try it. Sorry. Price
range: 25.4 oz, $1.99–2.39.

♀♀♀ LANGENBACH   MOSELBLUMCHEN   QUALITATSWEIN
Product of Langenbach & Company, Worms am
Rhein, Germany. Rating: 10. Distribution: B. This
pale, blonde wine has a slightly reluctant nose, but
when it does come through you get a mixture of spice
and fruit, nicely blended but offered with restraint.
The spiciness is confirmed in the mouth, where the
wine comes off clean and cheerful, semidry with just a
touch of fruit sweetness. All in all, it's a very amiable
wine. Price range: 34 oz, $2.59–2.99.

♀♀♀♀ LEONARD KREUSCH LIEBFRAUMILCH   Produced &
bottled by Leonard Kreusch, Trier, Germany. Rating:
12. Distribution: B. This is a charming wine, lithe,
supple, rounded, and totally enjoyable. The color is
clean and sunny. The nose is soft and clean, moderately fruity, and the taste is light, healthy, ripe,
feminine, delightful, and pleasingly sweet. Try a
bottle if you can find it, and I hope you can! Price
range: 23 oz, $2.55–3.19.

♀ LIBERTY SCHOOL NAPA VALLEY WHITE WINE   Produced
& bottled by Caymus Vineyards, Rutherford, California. Rating: 8+. Distribution: C. This light, clear
wine has an assertive nose that is lean and masculine
without making a big deal of it. It's upright and
authoritative with a touch of fruit held well back. The

taste is also somewhat restrained, but offers more than the nose. It's a slender wine, thoughty rather than voluptuous, semidry, with a slight stalkiness. There's an interesting aftertaste, rather pleasant, of fruit, weeds, herbs, stalks, what have you. Price range: 25.6 oz, $2.95–3.25.

LOPE DE VEGA BLANCO   Elaborado y criado por Vinicola Iberica, S.A., Tarragona, Spain. Rating: 7+. Distribution: C. The color is brilliant, clean, golden with hints of olive. The nose is somber and quiet, with no particular excitement or "come hither." The taste is tart, dry, refreshing, and somewhat unusual in having a sort of birchbark or herbal component, but it's not so interesting or memorable that you'll want to put the wine terribly high on your list. Price range: 24 oz, $1.19–1.39.

♀♀ LOS HERMANOS CALIFORNIA CHABLIS   Made & bottled by Los Hermanos Vineyards, St. Helena, California. Rating: 9. Distribution: A. There is a quiet fruitiness in the modest aroma of this Chablis. It's clean and round, and the flavor echoes these harmonious characteristics. It has a modest sweetness amid the fruit, and it's a very congenial, enjoyable wine. Price range: 50.7 oz, $2.99–3.49.

♀♀♀ LOS HERMANOS CALIFORNIA CHARDONNAY   Made & bottled by Los Hermanos Vineyards, St. Helena, California. Rating: 10. Distribution: A. There are faint green lights in the amber color of this Chardonnay. The nose is assertive, zesty, youthful, just barely ripe. The taste is attractively dry, tart and racy, with tons of fresh fruit peeking through, reminding you of sunny days and dancing on the lawn. Price range: 50.7 oz, $3.39–3.99.

♀ LOS HERMANOS CALIFORNIA CHENIN BLANC Made & bottled by Los Hermanos Vineyards, St. Helena, California. Rating: 8+. Distribution: A. This Chenin Blanc has a mild, decent aroma and a mild, sweet slightly flat taste. There is some fruit in both the nose and mouth, and at its price, it's not a bad wine. Price range: 50.7 oz, $3.19–3.69.

♀♀♀ LOS HERMANOS CALIFORNIA JOHANNISBERG RIESLING Made & bottled by Los Hermanos Vineyards, St. Helena, California. Rating: 10+. Distribution: A. Color: pale, straw, tawny cast. Nose: vigorous, fruity, fresh, crisp. Taste: semidry, rich fruit flavors, pleasing natural fruit sweetness, smooth, supple, very drinkable. Give it a try. Price range: 50.7 oz, $3.19–3.69.

MANISCHEWITZ CREAM WHITE CONCORD Produced & bottled by Manischewitz Wine Company, New York, New York. Rating: 5. Distribution: B. This is a pale, delicate wine to look at, and that's about where it stops. There's a touch of old rubber tires in the nose, and that spoils everything else. Its other characteristics, some of which could have been sweet and charming, all get submerged in the aroma and taste of an ancient inner tube. Price range: 25.6 oz, $2.19–2.49.

MARQUÉS DEL LAGAR VINO BLANCO From Bodegas Marqués del Lagar, Logroño, Spain. Rating: 4. Distribution: C. Very bad. An aroma of dirty sweat socks, a similar experience in the mouth. Sloppily made, old, tired, unkempt, etc., etc. Price range: 24 oz, $2.29–2.59.

♀ LOUIS M. MARTINI CALIFORNIA MOUNTAIN CHABLIS Produced & bottled by Louis M. Martini, St. Helena, California. Rating: 8. Distribution: B. This Chablis has a deep color, gold and handsome. The nose is unusual for a Chablis, and so is the taste, although California Chablis can vary all over the lot. This nose is clean, heavy, and makes me think they made the wine from apples, not grapes. The taste is a refreshing sweet-and-sour combination, slightly heavy, and I kept thinking of iced tea as I tasted it. Nice, but different. Price range: 25.6 oz, $2.25–2.69.

LOUIS M. MARTINI CALIFORNIA MOUNTAIN DRY SAUTERNE Produced & bottled by Louis M. Martini, St. Helena, California. Rating: 7+. Distribution: B. Adequate is the word for this wine. It's lovely and clear to look at, but the nose is a bit stuffy, and the taste follows right along in the same vein: dour, the fruitiness restrained, deficient in charm, vigor, and excitement. Adequate, nothing more. Price range: 25.6 oz, $2.25–2.69.

♀♀♀ LOUIS M. MARTINI CALIFORNIA MOUNTAIN WHITE WINE CHABLIS Prepared & bottled by Louis M. Martini, St. Helena, California. Rating: 10. Distribution: B. In a sense this is a small-scale wine, because it doesn't really excell in any single quality. Still, the way it's put together, and the total sensation of eye, nose, mouth, and brain makes it worthwhile. The color is wheat. The nose is iced tea with fruit. The taste is light, dryish, pleasantly tart, straightforward, well balanced. It's not complex, but it's well integrated, and it's worth your trouble to try a bottle. Price range: 25.6 oz, $1.75–2.39.

♀♀ PAUL MASSON CALIFORNIA CHABLIS   Made & bottled by Paul Masson Vineyards, Saratoga, California. Rating: 9+. Distribution: A. This Chablis has a straightforward nose, a bit hard, with pleasant fruit and a nice, clean feeling overall. The taste is gently sweet, and the fruit comes through, clean and ripe. All the parts seem nicely assembled, including the agreeably refreshing acid balance, and you'll probably like it. Price range: 25.4 oz, $2.15–2.39.

♀♀ PAUL MASSON CALIFORNIA CHENIN BLANC   Produced & bottled by Paul Masson Vineyards, Saratoga, California. Rating: 9. Distribution: A. This wine has a deep, rich hue, somewhat akin to a medium-dry Sherry. The nose is middle of the road, quite acceptable but nothing special. In the mouth it's sunny and agreeable. I could use a little more acid in its balance, but it's plenty attractive as it stands. Price range: 25.4 oz, $2.69–2.99.

♀ PAUL MASSON CALIFORNIA RHINE   Produced & bottled by Paul Masson Vineyards, Saratoga, California. Rating: 8. Distribution: A. There are faint olive touches in the pale gold of this wine, and the effect is handsome. The nose is a bit stuffy, and makes me think of rooms that haven't been opened for a long time. The taste is a modest offering, not sweet, not dry, refreshing in its way, but with a small touch of bitterness in the backtaste. Better than middle of the road, but still a ways to go. Price range: 25.4 oz, $2.15–2.39.

PAUL MASSON CALIFORNIA SAUTERNE CHÂTEAU MASSON Made & bottled by Paul Masson Vineyards, Saratoga, California. Rating: 6. Distribution: A. The color is deep and rich, like a French Sauterne. The nose is aggressive, heavy, strident, weedy. The same characteristics turn up in the taste. The heavy, strident tones combine with a syrupy sweetness to make this wine something less than desirable, I'm afraid. Price range: 25.4 oz, $2.39–2.69.

ҀҀҀ PAUL MASSON EMERALD DRY WHITE TABLE WINE Produced & bottled by Paul Masson Vineyards, Saratoga, California. Rating: 11. Distribution: A. The color: pale straw. The nose: assertive, crisp, clean, delightful, lots of fruit. The taste: fruit, some sweetness, well balanced, cheerful, bracing, pleasing aftertaste. Conclusion: It's a good wine to remember! Price range: 25.4 oz, $2.39–2.69.

ҀҀҀҀ PAUL MASSON RHINE CASTLE Produced & bottled by Paul Masson Vineyards, Saratoga, California. Rating: 11+. Distribution: A. Color: clean, handsome, golden. Aroma: powerful, fruity, sweet, racy, fresh, full of apples, grapes, mangoes. Taste: full of fruit, sweet, almost thick, more like a sweet Sauterne than a Rhine, a good wine to accompany a sweet dessert, but not to be served with the Sole Marguery. As has been said of other specialized wines, "Of its kind, extraordinarily nice." Price range: 25.4 oz, $2.39–2.69.

MAZZOLINI SOAVE Produced & bottled by Giuliano & Donato Mazzolini, Cremona, Italy. Rating: 7+. Dis-

tribution: C. This wine has a color so deep and golden
it's almost thick. The nose is assertive with the
freshness of newly mown green grass, and I have to
say that it's a trifle too pungent for me. From the taste
I get a feeling that the wine was made in the vicinity
of a cider press, but what's wrong with that? All you
have to do is get used to the flavor. Because it's not
bad, it's just different. Price range: 24 oz, $1.39–1.79.

MIRASSOU MONTEREY–SANTA CLARA CHABLIS   Produced
& bottled by Mirassou Vineyards, San Jose, California. Rating: 7+. Distribution: B. This pale, clean wine
has an arid, dusty aroma, not unpleasant but just a bit
desiccated. The taste follows the nose in being a bit
bleak, overly reserved, holding back. There's fruit,
and it's decent and drinkable, but it somehow escapes
the touch of character or style that makes this type of
wine come off. Price range: 25.4 oz, $2.95–3.19.

MOGEN DAVID CREAM WHITE CONCORD   Bottled by
Mogen David Wine Corp., Chicago, Illinois. Rating:
7. Distribution: B. This white wine has a small,
assertive nose that is a little too pointed to be truly
inviting. In the mouth it's sweet, smooth, fruity,
almost a dessert wine, but with a slight taste of rubber
or petroleum. Not a whole lot of that taste, just a hint,
but enough to make you look elsewhere for the wine
of your dreams. Price range: 25.6 oz, $2.09–2.29.

♀♀ MOMMESSIN CUVÉE SAINT-PIERRE   Shipped by
Mommessin, Mâcon, France. Rating: 9. Distribution:
B. It's the color of very dry Sherry. The nose is clean,
decent, presentable, and the taste is dry, spare, stylish
in a lean sort of way, with just enough fruit to keep it
adult and dignified. Price range: 24 oz, $2.99–3.29.

♀♀ CK MONDAVI CALIFORNIA SELECT CHABLIS Made & bottled by C. Mondavi & Sons, St. Helena, California. Rating: 9+. Distribution: A. There are flowers and fruit in the delicate aroma of this pale Chablis. The nose is a bit bashful, but comes through enough to be enjoyable. The taste is modestly on the sweet side, light and amiable and floral, with a gentle acid balance. It's not a wine of great consequence, but it's very enjoyable. Give it a try. Price range: 25.4 oz, $1.59–1.89.

♀♀♀ CK MONDAVI CALIFORNIA SELECT DRY SAUTERNE Made & bottled by C. Mondavi & Sons, St. Helena, California. Rating: 10. Distribution: A. I think you'll like this one. It's the color of wheat, and the nose is clean, agreeable, and promises refreshment. The promise is kept in the mouth, where the wine is modestly dry, has enough fruit to be pleasing, and displays good balance. Price range: 25.4 oz, $1.59–1.89.

♀♀♀ CK MONDAVI CALIFORNIA SELECT RHINE Made & bottled by C. Mondavi & Sons, St. Helena, California. Rating: 10+. Distribution: A. Mondavi's Rhine has greenish tones in its color, and the pleasing freshness of just-ripe fruit in its nose. The balance between sweet and tart in the mouth strikes me as being just right, and the whole effect is one of sunshine, liveliness, simplicity, and just a tiny touch of spice. Nice. Price range: 25.4 oz, $1.59–1.89.

♀♀ ROBERT MONDAVI CALIFORNIA WHITE TABLE WINE Produced & bottled by Robert Mondavi Winery, Oakville, California. Rating: 9. Distribution: A. This is a nice, inconsequential wine that you'll probably enjoy. I get an aroma of iced tea in its modest nose, but in the mouth it's nothing like iced tea at all. It's light, cheerful, fruity, refreshing. It's not pretending to be anything but a friendly, enjoyable drink, and that's precisely what it is. Price range: 25.6 oz, $2.19–2.59.

NAVARIS WHITE WINE   Produced & bottled by the Union of Agricole Cooperatives of Vinegrowers of Thebes, Greece. Rating: 5. Distribution: C. The label is charming and carries the words "Pure Greek dry wine special grapes of Thebes," but it must have been shipped to the United States under the theory that the Americans will drink anything. It is a light, golden color, with considerable sediment. The aroma is common and weedy, the wine flabby, lacking in acid, with a touch of bitterness. Price range: 22 oz, $1.19–1.49.

NOVITIATE CALIFORNIA CHABLIS   Produced & bottled by Novitiate of Los Gatos, Los Gatos, California. Rating: 5. Distribution: C. This is a beautiful wine to look at—deep golden, dark, almost topaz. Unfortunately, it's not terribly good. The nose is heavy, assertive, and reminds me of bark stripped from green willows. The taste is dry, with lots of fruit but little delicacy. It's ponderous, clumsy, and disappointing. Price range: 25.6 oz, $2.50–2.99.

ƾƾƾ NOVITIATE CALIFORNIA PINOT BLANC   Produced & bottled by Novitiate of Los Gatos, Los Gatos, California. Rating: 10. Distribution: C. This is a clear, pale, green-gold wine with dignity. The nose is forthright and clean, with the kind of austerity one finds in a French Chablis. The taste is serious, restrained, mature, refined. It has style, and will probably appeal less to novices than to experienced wine bibbers. Price range: 25.6 oz, $2.99–3.50.

PAMPAS BLANCO Produced & bottled by Bodegas y Viñedos Lopez, Mendoza, Argentina. Rating: 5+. Distribution: C. The color is rich, like dull gold. The aroma is dour, pessimistic, medicinal. The taste, too, is herbal and medicinelike, and this all adds up to a wine that is definitely not my kind of wine experience. Price range: 24 oz, $1.19–1.39.

♀♀♀♀♀ ANGELO PAPAGNI CALIFORNIA MUSCAT ALEX-ANDRIA Produced & bottled by Papagni Vineyards, Madera, California. Rating: 13. Distribution: B. Lovely, gorgeous, fruity, sweet! It has a dry-sherry color and an ambrosial aroma, ripe and mature and full of flowers and fruit. In the mouth it's rich, thick, round and honeyed, full of fruit and fruit sweetness. It's an ode to summer, natural sugars, sunshine, dappled shade under mighty oaks, and if you're looking for healthy sensuality in a wine that's sweet, you just found it. Price range: 25.6 oz, $2.50–2.99.

♀ PARDUCCI CALIFORNIA CHABLIS Produced & bottled by Parducci Wine Cellars, Ukiah, California. Rating: 8+. Distribution: B. It's a beautiful rich gold color and gives promise of being wonderful. As it turns out, it's just a nice, slightly better than middle-of-the-road wine, pleasant, offering some fruit, but without surprises or complexity. Not terrible, not wonderful, just okay-plus. Price range: 25.6 oz, $2.50–3.10.

♀♀ PARDUCCI MENDOCINO COUNTY FRENCH COLOMBARD Produced & bottled by Parducci Wine Cellars,

Ukiah, California. Rating: 9+. Distribution: B. The aroma of this pale blonde Colombard is modest, but it's clean and acceptable. In the mouth, the wine picks up considerably, and the sensation is that of sugar and fruit and acid working nicely together to produce a slightly sweet, well-balanced wine. I think you may enjoy it. Price range: 25.6 oz, $2.50–3.10.

PEDRONCELLI SONOMA COUNTY CHABLIS   Produced & bottled by J. Pedroncelli Winery, Geyserville, California. Rating: 7+. Distribution: B. The color is pale and golden, the nose is modest and cheerful, with a faint scent of lemons. In the mouth the wine is thin and light, lacking in flavor and fruit, but if you chill it well, it will still brighten your dinner. Price range: 25.6 oz, $2.00–2.49.

♀♀ PEDRONCELLI SONOMA WHITE WINE   Bottled by J. Pedroncelli Winery, Geyserville, California. Rating: 9. Distribution: B. This wine has an amber cast, and a clean, agreeable, and somewhat modest nose. In the mouth it has a moderate sweetness, soft, with a cheerful supply of fruit. The general sensation is one of suppleness and relaxation, and you'll probably enjoy it. Price range: 25.6 oz, $1.59–1.79.

♀♀ PETRI CALIFORNIA CHABLIS BLANC   Produced & bottled by Petri Wineries, San Francisco, California. Rating: 9. Distribution: A. Petri's Chablis is modest, unassuming, but very satisfying. The color is very light, slightly tawny, and the nose is clean, decent, forthright, sturdy rather than delicate. The taste is semisweet, light, innocent, with a good supply of fruit, and good balance. There's a slight feeling of restraint in the wine, as though it could give more if it really tried, but what it gives is really good enough for a lot of occasions. Price range: 25.6 oz, $.99–1.39.

♀♀ PETRI CALIFORNIA SAUTERNE   Produced & bottled by Petri Wineries, San Francisco, California. Rating: 9+. Distribution: A. This is a pale, clear wine with a nose that is somewhat reluctant, but warm, fruity, and genial. The taste is semidry, and there is a good show of fruit. It's a bit astringent, but that makes it lively and athletic. You may sense a slight backtaste, but it's minimal, so you might as well go ahead and enjoy it. After all, the price is right! Price range: 25.6 oz, $.99–1.39.

♀♀ RABIER BLANC DE BLANCS   Shipped by G. Rabier & Fils, Loir & Cher, France. Rating: 9. Distribution: C. The color is slightly tawny. The nose is a bit shy, but warm, rounded, and lightly floral. The taste is semidry, fresh, lively, with a pleasing tart edge, and just enough sweetness to make it satisfying. It's an energetic wine, a congenial wine, and if someone near you has a bottle, buy it! Price range: 24 oz, $2.39–2.89.

RICASOLI SOAVE DRY WHITE WINE   Produced & bottled at Cantina Sociale Valtramigna, Verona, Italy. Rating: 5+. Distribution: B. This handsome bottle of wine just doesn't make it, friends, and no one is sorrier than I. The nose is old, withered, woody, and just doesn't make you eager for another sniff. The taste confirms the aroma. It's not just dry, it's sourish, with a woody, resiny aftertaste. And such a handsome bottle! Price range: 24 oz, $2.99–3.29.

RIUNITE BIANCO   Produced & bottled by Cantine Coop., Riunite, Reggio Emilia, Italy. Rating: 7+. Distribution: A. The television commercials are compelling, but the wine is very ordinary. The color is terrific—a deep, rich amber with a gold rim. The nose is ponderous, clumsy, slightly cooked, and the taste has the same baked character. It's not a bad wine—it has a clean, semisweet taste and a fair quantity of fruit—but it's just not an experience you'll want to have over and over. Price range: 24 oz, $2.39–2.59.

ROCAFLOR VIN BLANC   Bottled by Union des Caves du Canton de Ginestas en Minervois (Aude) France. Rating: 6. Distribution: C. Rocaflor Vin Blanc is a sunny, golden wine that promises much and delivers little. The aroma has no class, no appeal. The wine itself is not badly made, but it's not well made, either. It has a rather sugary palate, and a touch of bitterness in the finish. Price range: 24 oz, $1.59–1.99.

SAN MARTIN CALIFORNIA MOUNTAIN CHABLIS   Produced & bottled by San Martin Vineyards, San Martin, California. Rating: 7. Distribution: B. The color is moderately deep, a sort of greenish gold. The nose is not terribly exciting, perhaps a little close. The taste is acceptable, semidry, with adequate fruit, but somehow the closed-in feeling of the nose gets translated into a similar feeling in the mouth. The result, while not awful, is run of the mill. Price range: 25.6 oz, $1.69–1.99.

SEBASTIANI NORTH COAST COUNTIES CHABLIS   Produced & bottled by Sebastiani Vineyards, Sonoma, California. Rating: 7 +. Distribution: A. Sebastiani's Chablis is the color of dry Sherry. There's a faint hint of sweetness in the slightly flowery nose, but that's pretty much where it ends. The wine tastes thin and flat, and there's a slightly bitter aftertaste. Sorry. Price range: 25.4 oz, $1.99–2.59.

♀ SEBASTIANI NORTH COAST COUNTIES GREEN HUN-GARIAN   Produced & bottled by Sebastiani Vineyards, Sonoma, California. Rating: 8+. Distribution: A. No two Green Hungarians are alike. This one is light in color, with hints of green, and has an honest nose, containing a fair amount of fruit. In the mouth I get spice, brier, and something that reminds me of the woodruff the Germans put into May wine. It's well balanced, has some sweetness, and seems well made. Price range: 25.4 oz, $2.50–2.79.

SEBASTIANI NORTH COAST COUNTIES SYLVANER RIES-LING   Produced & bottled by Sebastiani Vineyards, Sonoma, California. Rating: 7. Distribution: A. There is a slight medicinal quality to the nose and taste of this wine, and it doesn't contribute to the success of the wine. The aroma is clean enough, no swampi-ness, and the taste isn't bad, but the tinge of camphor or cedar chest is just too much in the foreground. Price range: 25.4 oz, $2.50–2.79.

♀♀SEBASTIANI NORTHERN CALIFORNIA CHENIN BLANC Produced & bottled by Sebastiani Vineyards, Sono-ma, California. Rating: 9. Distribution: A. This Che-nin Blanc has a light, clear color, and a shy aroma. If you sniff hard enough, you'll come on a few floral attributes that are rather pleasing. In the mouth the wine is on the sweet side of the Chenin Blanc spec-trum, with fruit and sugar aplenty. A little more acid would help, but it's still a very nice bottle of wine. Price range: 25.4 oz, $2.50–2.79.

SEBASTIANI NORTHERN CALIFORNIA MOUNTAIN CHAB-
LIS Made & bottled by Sebastiani Vineyards, Sonoma, California. Rating: 6. Distribution: A. Not much
here except the lovely ripe-wheat color. The nose is a
bit foreboding, and the taste is clumsy, mechanical,
resiny, and lacking in any kind of delight or jollity.
Price range: 25.4 oz, $1.60–1.99.

♀♀♀ SEBASTIANI NORTHERN CALIFORNIA MOUNTAIN
PINOT CHARDONNAY Made & bottled by Sebastiani
Vineyards, Sonoma, California. Rating: 10. Distribution: A. This wine has a cultivated nose with a sense
of maturity and serenity. It won't knock you over with
its fruitiness or its energy, because it has better
manners than that. The taste is semidry, restrained,
sweet-sour. The fruit is there, clean and inviting, and
the net effect is somehow healthy and cultivated, yet
sedate, and very pleasing. Price range: 25.4 oz,
$2.59–2.89.

♀♀ SEGESTA WHITE DRY TABLE WINE Produced & bottled by Diego Rallo & Figli, Marsala, Italy. Rating: 9.
Distribution: B. The color is pale and greenish, the
nose is very formal, almost to the point of stuffiness.
The whole feeling of the wine is one of restraint and
dignity. The taste is dry, serious, and somehow
related to the taste of French Chablis. It's not a "wine
for lovers," because it's really intended to be drunk by
wise old Italian men as they play bocce ball. Price
range: 24 oz, $2.99–3.49.

♀♀ SETRAKIAN MOUNTAIN WHITE CHABLIS Produced &
bottled by Robert Setrakian Vineyards, Yettem, California. Rating: 9. Distribution: B. Setrakian's Chablis

is an attractive straw color, and the aroma, while not overpowering, is pleasant and floral. The wine has some sweetness in the mouth, could use a trace more acid to perk it up, but on the whole it is an amiable, undemanding, enjoyable white wine, and I recommend that you find a bottle and try it. Price range: 25.6 oz, $1.39–1.69.

SONOMA VINEYARDS CALIFORNIA FRENCH COLOMBARD Produced & bottled by Sonoma Vineyards, Windsor, California. Rating: 7. Distribution: B. There is an unfortunate cistern quality to the aroma of this good-looking Colombard, and it keeps it from scoring the way it otherwise should. There's fruit and a certain rounded quality in the taste, but the staleness of the nose keeps intruding, and detracts from the total sensation. Price range: 25.4 oz, $2.39–2.89.

SONOMA VINEYARDS SONOMA COUNTY CHENIN BLANC Produced & bottled by Sonoma Vineyards, Windsor, California. Rating: 7+. Distribution: B. Noses are funny things. Some foretell what will happen when you get the wine in your mouth. Some hide it from you. This Chenin Blanc is of the former variety, because there is a bit of stridency in the nose that telegraphs a message about the somewhat coarse taste. It's a rude peasant flavor, with stems, bark and all to keep you from your simple enjoyment of the fruit. Price range: 25.4 oz, $2.59–3.19.

SOUVERAIN OF ALEXANDER VALLEY MENDOCINO GREY RIESLING Produced & bottled by Souverain, Geyserville, California. Rating: 7+. Distribution: B. The color is pale and wan, the nose is not very fetching.

The taste is dry and austere, and despite having some fruit and a few somewhat classic touches, is really a middle-of-the-roader. It's a bit ascetic—no, not acetic; ascetic—and I have an idea it may be drunk by an order of very devout monks. The jolly monks drink something else. Price range: 25.6 oz, $2.50–2.99.

♀♀♀ SOUVERAIN OF ALEXANDER VALLEY NORTH COAST DRY CHENIN BLANC   Produced & bottled by Souverain, Geyserville, California. Rating: 10+. Distribution: B. This Souverain wine has a nice aroma and taste. The character is a bit austere, but that's okay; sometimes we get tired of jolly wines. The nose is simple and dignified, and the taste is full, dry, rounded, and satisfying. Overall, it's a nice, reserved sort of wine with just enough fruit and sprightliness to keep it from being dull. I think you may like it. Price range: 25.6 oz, $2.75–3.29.

STELLENRYCK RIESLING   Produced by Die Bergkelder, Stellenbosch, Republic of South Africa. Rating: 7+. Distribution: C. This pale, straw-colored wine has one of the greatest labels you ever saw. That's a principal reason why it's so disappointing that the wine, imported all the way from South Africa, isn't better. The nose is definite but not very appealing, the wine itself is dry, stolid, interesting in its unmistakable character, but nevertheless not likely to become one of your favorites. It's a pity. Price range: 24 oz, $1.59–2.39.

STELLENRYCK STEIN   Produced by Die Bergkelder, Stellenbosch, Republic of South Africa. Rating: 7+. Distribution: C. This South African import, like its sister Riesling, has its own definite personality, but it's not a personality I like very much. The color is golden, slightly murky (so is the Riesling), and the aroma is straightforward, if a bit harsh and lacking in charm. The wine is sweeter than the Riesling, on the heavy side, and has a trace of bitterness in the finish. I get a feeling of earnest gracelessness. Price range: 24 oz, $1.59–2.39.

♀♀♀ STERLING NAPA VALLEY WHITE TABLE WINE   Bottled by Sterling Vineyards, Calistoga, California. Rating: 10. Distribution: B. This light, tawny wine has a slender but very pleasing bouquet that displays some fruit and somehow seemed to me to have a hint of licorice in it. The taste is rounded, full, feminine, and ingratiating. There's a nice balance of natural acidity and fruit, and the result may please your palate as it did mine: Price range: 25.6 oz, $2.49–2.99.

SUMMIT CHABLIS   Cellared & bottled by Geyser Peak Winery, Geyserville, California. Rating: 7+. Distribution: B. Summit's Chablis has very little color, and a somewhat thin nose that includes a whiff of something akin to varnish. The aroma is not really awful, it's just not terribly good, and the same is true of the taste. There's nothing really wrong; it's just commonplace, unexciting, ordinary white wine. Price range: 25.4 oz, $1.99–2.29.

♀ TAKARA-GREIF WHITE LIGHT WINE   Produced & bottled by Takara Shuzo Co., Ltd., Tokyo, Japan. Rating: 8. Distribution: C. This Japanese import, billed as a "white light wine," is not light in any way. The color is very dark, a deep amber color, the nose is heavy and has a sort of caramel aroma, and the taste is smooth, sweet, almost syrupy. As a table wine it's not very appealing, but as a sweet dessert wine, it's very nice, something like a Port. Thus, its 8 rating comes from its after-dinner qualities alone. Price range: 18.6 oz, $.99–1.19.

♀ TAYLOR NEW YORK STATE SAUTERNE Produced & bottled by Taylor Wine Co., Hammondsport, New York. Rating: 8+. Distribution: B. This is a nice, acceptable, middle-aged wine, decent and unremarkable, but not exactly brimming over with excitement. The nose has slight floral accents, and the taste is a bit flat, a bit on the sweet side, with some fruit, but without zest. The sunniest thing about it is its color, which is nice and bright and attractive. Price range: 25.4 oz, $2.15–2.49.

♈♈ TORRES SAN VALENTÍN Produced & bottled by Miguel Torres, Vilafranca del Panades, Spain, Rating: 9. Distribution: B. This pale, clear wine has a simple, open aroma with some fruitiness. The taste is sweet, full bodied, uncomplicated, with an agreeable fruitiness. If you're looking for a sweet table wine, give this one a try. Price range: 24 oz, $2.49–2.79.

TORRES VIÑA SOL Produced & bottled by Miguel Torres, Vilafranca del Panadés, Spain. Rating: 7+. Distribution: B. There are flecks of green in the sunny, golden color of this import from Spain. The nose is unobtrusive, amiable when located, and the taste is crisp, dry almost to the point of sourness, with an astringency that some may like, but I translate as unripeness. Price range: 24 oz, $2.49–2.79.

♀ UVITA CHABLIS Produced & bottled by Dobboletta & Cia., S.A. Mendoza, Argentina. Rating: 8. Distribution: C. There is a deep, golden color of autumn sunshine in the look of this wine, and there is a unique, piquant touch of citrus and herbs in the bouquet. In a way it's almost like a May wine, with its touch of woodruff, and it's rather enjoyable. It's a bit too medicinal and barky to drink too often, however, but now and again you might enjoy a glass or two, just for a change. Price range: 24 oz, $.99–1.39.

♈♈ VILLA BANFI ROMAN WHITE Produced & bottled by C.A.C.S., Arricia (Roma) Italy. Rating: 9. Distribution: B. The color is a delicate pale green. The nose is shy but clean, with fruit lurking in the background. The taste is light, clean, pleasant, refreshing, and somewhat sedate. It's a cultivated wine, not a jolly one, and it's very decent. Try it. Price range: 24 oz, $1.99–2.49.

♈♈ VILLA MARIA SOAVE Bottled & shipped by CA. VI. SA., Verona, Italy. Rating: 9. Distribution: B. This Italian import has a honeyed golden color with flashes of green. The nose is decent, a bit shy, and shows a modest fruitiness. The taste is somewhat unusual, and has a number of pleasing flavors—apricots, cider, iced tea—that may not appeal to the classicists, but you and I are at liberty to enjoy them as much as we want. Modestly sweet, incidentally. Price range: 50 oz, $3.49–3.99.

VIÑA UNDURRAGA GRAN VINO RHIN Produced & bottled by Viña Undurraga, Estacion Sta. Ana, Chile. Rating: 5+. Distribution: C. I had hoped this wine would turn out to be as charming as the squat little bottle it came in, but alas, the contents were thin, watery, and corky. The aroma seemed a little spoiled and stemmy, and the aftertaste was a bit bitter. It's drinkable, but it won't be much of an addition to your dinner. Price range: 24 oz, $.99–1.09.

ΨΨ WEIBEL CALIFORNIA CLASSIC CHABLIS   Produced & bottled by Weibel Champagne Vineyards, Mission San Jose, California. Rating: 9. Distribution: C. Pale straw color, simple, fruity aroma. An attractive wine with an agreeable degree of sweetness that is nicely balanced with acid. In all, it has a considerable amount of charm without trying too hard to be more than a well-made, nicely fresh, white wine. Price range: 25.6 oz, $1.99–2.39.

ΨΨ WEIBEL CALIFORNIA GREEN HUNGARIAN   Produced & bottled by Weibel Champagne Vineyards, Mission San Jose, California. Rating: 9. Distribution: C. This Green Hungarian has a fair amount of sweetness, but for a sweet wine (if that's your thing) it's quite nice. It has a light honey color, and the nose is acceptable, if a bit on the underripe side. In the mouth it's a somewhat heavy wine, with a bouquet of flowers and iced tea. Orange pekoe, I think. The overall sensation is pleasing, assuming that a sweet wine is what you like. Price range: 25.6 oz, $2.69–2.99.

ΨΨΨΨ WEIBEL   CALIFORNIA   HOFFBERG   MAY   WINE Produced & bottled by Weibel Champagne Vineyards, Mission San Jose, California. Rating: 11+. Distribution: C. If you're a May-wine freak, and many of us are, Weibel's Hoffberg is one you must try. It's a dark amber color with gold flecks, and the aroma is almost mystical. Naturally, as with all May wines, it's herbal, but it's also very clean, and conjures up images of bazaars, sultans, and exotic fruit. The taste is smooth, warm (even when served cold, as it should be), sweet, rounded, woodsy, and if a lovely Persian princess doesn't materialize as you're drinking it (or prince, as the case may be), I'll be surprised. Price range: 25.6 oz, $1.99–2.49.

♀♀♀ WENTE BROTHERS CALIFORNIA CHABLIS   Produced & bottled by Wente Brothers, Livermore, California. Rating: 11. Distribution: B. One of the good ones. A nice clear wine the color of ripe wheat, with a full, rounded aroma that makes me think of lemon trees. In the mouth you'll find fruit, flowers—lemon blossoms, maybe—and a pleasant touch of sweetness, thankfully not a very heavy touch. It's a nice wine; try it. Price range: 25.6 oz, $2.15–2.59.

♀♀ WENTE BROTHERS CALIFORNIA GREY RIESLING Produced & bottled by Wente Bros. Winery, Livermore, California. Rating: 9. Distribution: B. Wente's celebrated Grey Riesling is a nice wine, and I like it, but I wish it could be even better. The taste is clean, fruity, and engaging, nicely refreshing in its balance, on the dry side, but the nose is hollow, and doesn't display much to get excited about. So, it's a good wine, a wine you will enjoy but think how you would have enjoyed it if it had a nose! Price range: 25.6 oz, $2.75–3.29.

♀ WIDMER NEW YORK STATE CANANDAIGUA LAKE NIAGARA   Produced & bottled by Widmer's Wine Cellars, Naples, New York. Rating: 8+. Distribution: C. The color is so light it's almost washed out entirely. The aroma is light, pleasing, clean, slightly floral. The taste is a bit on the sweet side, a bit unusual to boot, and it will probably appeal most to tastes that have already been educated to it. It's a nice wine, a well-made wine, and an enjoyable wine, but don't expect jollity or sophistication. Price range: 25.6 oz, $2.39–2.69.

WIDMER NEW YORK STATE DRY SAUTERNE   Produced & bottled by Widmer's Wine Cellars, Naples, New York. Rating: 7. Distribution: C. It's straw colored, and I also sense some hay or straw in both the aroma and the taste. It's a sort of mustiness, a closed-in, slightly stuffy characteristic. It's not terrible, but it gets in the way of all the good things in the wine. Not a bad wine, but another that rides down the center stripe of the highway. Price range: 25.6 oz, $2.35–2.59.

♈ WINEMASTERS CALIFORNIA CHENIN BLANC   Made & bottled by Winemasters' Guild, San Francisco, California. Rating: 9+. Distribution: A. This pale, silvery gold wine has a decent, small-scale nose that makes me think of fruit in a dusty vineyard. In the mouth the wine is smooth and supple with a modest sweetness, pleasing fruitiness, and a delicate acid balance. It has a restrained femininity that is very attractive, and I think you'll like it. Price range: 25.6 oz, $1.89–2.19.

♈ WINEMASTERS CALIFORNIA FRENCH COLOMBARD Made & bottled by The Winemasters' Guild, San Francisco, California. Rating: 9+. Distribution: A. This wine has an engaging honey color, and a shy, clean nose that offers occasional floral overtones. In the mouth, the wine seems well put together, with a refreshing balance of fruit and acid, and a little hint of something agreeably spicy in the background. I like it; maybe you will, too. Price range: 25.4 oz, $1.89–2.19.

WINEMASTERS CALIFORNIA GREEN HUNGARIAN Made & bottled by The Winemasters' Guild, San Francisco, California. Rating: 7+. Distribution: A. It's amber in color, clear, and has a slightly baked nose. Not bad, just a hot weather aroma that's not terrible, but isn't all that wonderful, either. In the mouth it has some fruit to show, but it seems a little bit thin and a little bit flat. Price range: 25.4 oz, $1.89–2.19.

ΨΨΨ WINEMASTERS CALIFORNIA JOHANNISBERG RIESLING Made & bottled by Winemasters' Guild, San Francisco, California. Rating: 10. Distribution: A. The color is light and clear, with a faint greenish cast. The nose is a bit shy, quietly fruity, and the taste is moderately sweet, inviting, velvety, refreshing, replete with feminine charms, and in no way shy. The fruit comes through nicely, and the whole effect is very pleasing. Price range: 25.6 oz, $2.49–2.79.

WINEMASTERS CALIFORNIA MOUNTAIN CHABLIS Made & bottled by Winemasters' Guild, San Francisco, California. Rating: 7+. Distribution: A. This is a very pale, watery-looking wine with a presentable, unremarkable nose that has no defects and a small sensation of fruit. The taste is either sweetly tart or tartly sweet, there's fruit and refreshment, but I doubt that you'll want to promote it from midweek to weekend. Price range: 25.6 oz, $1.69–1.99.

WINEMASTERS CALIFORNIA WHITE BURGUNDY Made & bottled by Winemasters' Guild, San Francisco, California. Rating: 7+. Distribution: A. The color: light, clear, silvery gold. The nose is decent but unextraordinary, with a touch of the closed-window syndrome. The taste: semidry, reserved, masculine, restrained fruit, slightly intellectual, slightly boring. Price range: 25.6 oz, $1.89–2.19.

ɣɣɣ WINEMASTERS GEWÜRZTRAMINER Made & bottled by Cave Cooperative d'Eguisheim, Alsace, France. Rating: 10+. Distribution: A. Not everybody likes the spiciness of a Gewürztraminer, but I think almost anyone could like this one. It's an attractive amber color, and it has a feminine, nicely fruity, honeyed nose that I found quite agreeable. In the mouth you get some traces of the spicy Gewürz flavor, but they seem to go along nicely with the rest of the structure. It's certainly very much worth your giving it a try. Price range: 24 oz, $1.99–2.59.

9

Pink Wines

ALMADÉN CALIFORNIA MOUNTAIN NECTAR VIN ROSÉ
Made & bottled by Almadén Vineyards, Los Gatos,
California. Rating: 5. Distribution: A. Vin Rosé is not
a subject on which I tend to wax enthusiastic, principally because there seem to be so few good ones. This
one by Almadén seems to prove the point, in that it
seems to have been made by a confectioner rather
than a vintner. The nose has a processed aroma, the
wine itself, light in color with orange tones, is flat,
dull, and syrupy. Price range: 25.6 oz, $1.79–2.10.

♀♀ BEAULIEU BEAUROSÉ Produced & bottled by Beaulieu Vineyards, Rutherford, California. Rating: 9.
Distribution: B. This brilliantly clear, crimson wine
has a clean, simple nose and a dry, thin, uncomplicated taste. It has fruit, and it has a cheerfully fresh
balance, and if rosé wines are your dish, this is one
you ought to try. Price range: 25.6 oz, $2.99–3.19.

♀ BEAULIEU VINEYARD CALIFORNIA GRENACHE ROSÉ
Produced & bottled by Beaulieu Vineyard, Rutherford, California. Rating: 8+. Distribution: B. Beaulieu has put together a light-hearted rosé that tastes like wine, not candy, and you might like it. The color is clean and pink with orange hints; the nose, while not overwhelming, is nevertheless pleasant enough, and the wine is enjoyably crisp and fruity in the mouth. Naturally, it has some sweetness, but it's nicely balanced with the other components. Price range: 25.6 oz, $2.49–2.75.

BERINGER NORTH COAST GAMAY ROSÉ   Produced & bottled by Beringer/Los Hermanos Vineyards, St. Helena, California. Rating: 7+. Distribution: A. The color is a lovely clear crimson. The nose is reluctant, decent, but hasn't a lot to say. In the mouth the wine doesn't offer a great deal, either. It's dryish with some fruit, and a little dull. I have the sense of its having met the qualifications for a vin rosé, but not gone beyond the minimums. Price range: 25.6 oz, $2.35–2.69.

BRONCO CALIFORNIA VIN ROSÉ   Cellared & bottled by Bronco Winery, Ceres, California. Rating: 6+. Distribution: C. There are tones of orange in this handsome vin rosé. The aroma has no particular defect, but nothing special to offer, either. In the mouth the wine is a cousin to sweet, flat soda pop. If it were well chilled, you might enjoy gulping some after a tennis match on a hot summer day. Outside of that, you might as well ignore it. Price range: 32 oz, $.99–1.19.

CABERNET D'ANJOU Bottled by Domaine Rahard, France. Rating: 7. Distribution: C. The color is a clear, beautiful orange. The nose is swampy and dank. The taste is slightly sweetish and slightly swampy. Nothing you want to go out searching for. Price range: 24 oz, $1.50–1.79.

CARLO ROSSI'S RED MOUNTAIN CALIFORNIA VIN ROSÉ Made & bottled by Carlo Rossi Vineyards, Modesto, California. Rating: 6. Distribution: A. Not very attractive, I'm afraid. The nose brings to mind old automobile tires, which carries over into the taste. It's not a total loss, because there is fruit present, and refreshment, but it's hard to take advantage of them with this unfortunate tire-shop component present. Price range: 25.4 oz, $.99–1.25.

CARMEL ROSÉ OF CARMEL Produced & bottled by Carmel Wine Growers Cooperative, Richon le Zion, Zichron Jacob, Israel. Rating: 7+. Distribution: A. There is some fruitiness in the otherwise oldish nose of this imported pink wine. The taste is semidry, rather dilute, with a touch of hot weather in the taste. It's acceptable, but just not great. Color: orangy-pink. Price range: 25.6 oz, $2.05–2.49.

CASTELLER CAVIT ROSÉ TABLE WINE Produced & bottled by Cavit, Cantina Viticoltori, Trento, Italy. Rating: 5+. Distribution: C. This wine is a bit dark for a rosé, but handsome nevertheless. Unfortunately, that's where this wine's beauty ends. The aroma and flavor both have a staleness that renders the wine unattractive and uninviting. It's as though it had been made in the presence of huge piles of dirty laundry. Too bad—the label looks so promising! Price range: 23 oz, $1.19–1.49.

CHÂTEAU DE SEGRIES ROSÉ RHÔNE WINE Produced & bottled by Le Comte de Regis, Lirac, France. Rating: 6+. Distribution: C. The bottle in which this lovely reddish-orange wine comes is wrapped in tissue paper, which gives the wine an extra air of being something special, which, unfortunately, it isn't. What it is is a very dry, almost sour wine of rather considerable astringency. The aroma has a slight floral bloom to it, but the wine itself is too full of acid to add much pleasure to anything but a very highly flavored meal. Price range: 24 oz, $1.00–1.29.

♀♀♀ CHRISTIAN BROTHERS LASALLE ROSÉ Produced & bottled by the Christian Brothers, Napa, California. Rating: 10+. Distribution: A. The color is a brilliant scarlet, and the wine spritzes when you pour it. It keeps on spritzing in your mouth in a pleasantly carbonated way, and if you can think past the spritz you'll find a fruity sweetness, fresh and rounded and energetic. The nose is clean, crisp, slightly formal, and the total effect of the wine is unusual and charming. Price range: 25.4 oz, $2.49–2.89.

CHRISTIAN BROTHERS SELECT CALIFORNIA VIN ROSÉ Produced & bottled by The Christian Brothers, Napa, California. Rating: 7. Distribution: A. There is almost no bouquet to this vin rosé, nothing good, nothing bad. The taste is pleasant and harmless, with some fruitiness, but on the whole the wine is fairly flat and has a bitter overtone in the aftertaste. Price range: 25.4 oz, $2.15–2.39.

♀ CONCANNON VINEYARD CALIFORNIA ZINFANDEL ROSÉ Produced & bottled by Concannon Vineyard, Livermore, California. Rating: 8. Distribution: C. The color of this wine is a bit dark for a rosé, but it's a good-looking wine all the same. The nose is acceptable without being terribly inviting. In the mouth the wine is agreeable, on the dry side, clean, and refreshing. It's not exactly a "jolly" wine; I'd say it's adult and thoughtful, and perhaps you ought to test-hop it for yourself. Price range: 25.6 oz, $2.99–3.29.

FAMIGLIA CRIBARI CALIFORNIA VIN ROSÉ Made & bottled by B. Cribari & Sons, San Francisco, California. Rating: 7+. Distribution: A. This is a middle-of-the-road wine, a rosé of medium color, with a sweetish, rather ordinary nose, and a taste without any special character traits. Acceptable, enjoyable if you don't ask too much of it, but you'll never remember much about it. Price range: 25.4 oz, $1.29–1.49.

♀ DELICATO ESPECIALLY SELECTED CALIFORNIA VIN ROSÉ Produced & bottled by Delicato Vineyards, Manteca, California. Rating: 8+. Distribution: B. The nose is a little processed, but isn't really a bad nose. The taste is dryish and refreshing with a nice show of fruit, and the whole thing seems simple and honest and, by and large, quite enjoyable. Price range: 25.6 oz, $1.39–1.59.

FAISCA VIN ROSÉ Bottled by João Pires & Fos., Portugal. Rating: 5+. Distribution: C. The color is brilliant and handsome, the aroma seems to come from a refinery. What a shame. There is a trace of spiciness laced into both the aroma and the taste, but it is so definitely overpowered that the wine, which looks so great in the bottle and in the glass, is hardly anything you'll want to give a second try. Price range: 24 oz, $.99–1.19.

♀ FRANZIA CALIFORNIA GRENACHE ROSÉ   Made & bottled by Franzia Brothers, Ripon, California. Rating: 8. Distribution: B. This rosé is a rich, deep vermilion, almost dark enough to be a light red rather than a dark pink. The nose is shy, clean, pleasant enough, and the taste is sweet and fruity, adequately balanced, unsophisticated, not terribly memorable, but presentable enough to drink, well chilled, on a very hot summer afternoon. Price range: 25.6 oz, $.99–1.29.

GALLO CALIFORNIA PINK CHABLIS   Made & bottled at the Gallo Vineyards, Modesto, California. Rating: 6+. Distribution: A. The color of this pink wine is a bit on the thin side, and the aroma leaves me a bit depressed. It seems to me to be a smell that comes from the processing, not from the grape, but who am I to tell the very successful Gallo brothers how to make their wine? This one is a bit too sweet, a bit too flat, but well chilled on a hot afternoon or transformed into a sangría with lots of citrus, you and I will probably like it just fine. Price range: 25.4 oz, $1.29–1.69.

♀ GALLO PRIME VINEYARD CALIFORNIA VIN ROSÉ   Made & bottled by Gallo Vineyards, Modesto, California. Rating: 8. Distribution: A. There's lots of orange in the pink of this vin rosé. The nose is modest, clean, pleasing, and the taste is clean and simple, sweetish, fruity, somewhat off in the direction of a soft drink, but enjoyable in an ingenuous sort of way. Price range: 25.4 oz, $1.49–1.89.

GROWERS CALIFORNIA GRENACHE ROSÉ Produced & bottled by California Growers Winery, San Francisco, California. Rating: 7+. Distribution: A. The middle of the road is full of acceptable wines that are easily forgotten, and this is one. Medium color for a vin rosé, with tawny hints, this wine has an unremarkable but decent aroma and an acceptable taste. There is fruit in the taste, but there is also a mildly bitter touch in the background, and the wine is a bit flat. You'd never reject the wine if it were served as a house rosé, but you also wouldn't make a note to seek it out. Price range: 25.6 oz, $1.29–1.59.

GUASTI CALIFORNIA COLOMBARD ROSÉ Made & bottled by Guasti Vintners, Delano, California. Rating: 7+. Distribution: B. The color is a clear, clean pink with a touch of orange. The taste is a bit heavy for a pink wine, and a bit baked. The taste is hot-weather sweetish, simple, ordinary, and middle of the road. Price range: 25.6 oz, $1.49–1.69.

ΨΨΨ INGLENOOK NORTH COAST COUNTIES VINTAGE CAB-ERNET ROSÉ Produced & bottled by Inglenook Vine-yards, Rutherford, California. Rating: 11. Distribution: A. This is a light scarlet wine with the Cabernet weediness in both taste and smell. The nose has dignity, a touch of refinement, and a display of pleasing fruitiness, all of which comes through again when you drink it. It's dry, has good balance, an agreeable and very modest tartness, and all in all—especially for a rosé—it's a very enjoyable wine. Price range: 25.4 oz, $2.50–2.89.

ITALIAN SWISS COLONY CALIFORNIA GRENACHE ROSÉ Produced & bottled by Italian Swiss Colony, Asti, California. Rating: 6. Distribution: A. Vin rosés often head off in the direction of soda pop, which is precisely what this one does. Now, there's nothing wrong with soda pop, but if you pay for wine, you want wine. This one has faint tones of fruit and spice in the nose, but the taste is sweet, flat, and innocuous. Not much here. Price range: 25.6 oz, $1.39–1.69.

♀ KORBEL CALIFORNIA CHÂTEAU VIN ROSÉ Produced & bottled by F. Korbel & Bros., Guerneville, California. Rating: 8. Distribution: B. The color of this vin rosé is intense and lovely, rubylike. The nose is reluctant, but without defects, and the sensation in the mouth is very pleasant—light and astringent in an enjoyable way, with a moderate amount of fruitiness and a controlled sweetness that avoids the syrupy qualities of some vins rosés. Worth a try. Price range: 25.4 oz, $2.25–2.65.

♀ CHARLES KRUG CALIFORNIA VIN ROSÉ Produced & bottled by Charles Krug Winery, St. Helena, California. Rating: 8+. Distribution: B. This wine has an attractive taste, on the sweet side but balanced nicely enough to exude a bit of charm. The refreshment is marred only by a vegetable note in the aroma that keeps this otherwise pleasing wine from scoring higher. Still, it's not bad. Price range: 25.4 oz, $2.25–2.65.

LOS HERMANOS CALIFORNIA MOUNTAIN ROSÉ WINE
Cellared & bottled by Beringer/Los Hermanos Vineyards, St. Helena, California. Rating: 6+. Distribution: A. This wine hovers near the "average" mark,
with a medium color and an unspectacular nose that
seems a bit dank and heavy. In the mouth the wine
seems thin and tasteless, with a shadowy note of
bitterness. Not terrible, not wonderful, just wine.
Price range: 50.7 oz, $2.99–3.49.

ȲȲȲ MAISON JACQUIN VIE EN ROSÉ   Shipped by the
House of Jacquin, Tours, France. Rating: 10. Distribution: C. This light, orangy rosé has a shy, clean
nose that offers a modest fruitiness. The taste is
balanced between sweet and dry, and there's some
feeling of quality in the flavor, a sense of refinement
in the way the sweetness and acid combine to produce
a fresh, satisfying wine. Price range: 24 oz, $1.29–
1.79.

MANISCHEWITZ CREAM PINK CONCORD   Produced & bottled by Manischewitz Wine Co., New York, New
York. Rating: 5. Distribution: B. It wouldn't be fair to
evaluate this wine simply as a vin rosé, since it's really
a category all its own. The wine has a fiery, intense
orange color that I thought very handsome, but the
nose was straight out of a tire shop, and the taste was
sweet, syrupy, and flat. I realize that a love of very
sweet wines may be an acquired taste, so if that's your
thing, give this one a try, but don't say I didn't warn
you! Price range: 25.6 oz, $2.19–2.49.

Ȳ LOUIS M. MARTINI CALIFORNIA MOUNTAIN GAMAY
ROSÉ   Produced & bottled by Louis M. Martini, St.

Helena, California. Rating: 8. Distribution: B. Louis Martini's Gamay Rosé falls into the category of "if the people have just come in out of the sun, and the wine is well chilled, the people will think the wine is nectar." Blind-tasted in less dramatic circumstances, you'd have to say that this rosé is no great shakes—a reluctant nose, a dry, thin mouth experience, and really only slightly better than ordinary. Price range: 25.6 oz, $2.45–3.10.

LOUIS M. MARTINI CALIFORNIA MOUNTAIN VIN ROSÉ Prepared & bottled by Louis M. Martini, St. Helena, California. Rating: 7+. Distribution: B. This vin rosé is decent, on the dry side, uncomplicated, a bit thin, a bit flat. The nose is unremarkable, and I felt I detected a vegetable note. Not a bad wine, not a very good one, either. Price range: 25.6 oz, $1.75–2.39.

♀♀♀ PAUL MASSON CALIFORNIA ROSÉ Made & bottled by Paul Masson Vineyards, Saratoga, California. Rating: 10. Distribution: A. This rosé is very pale, with a clear, fruity, rounded aroma. The taste is on the sweet side, healthy, youthful, full of fruit, and quite enjoyable. The acid balance is modest but adequate, and if you're a rosé fancier, this is a candidate for your next taste-test. Price range: 25.4 oz, $2.15–2.39.

PAUL MASSON CALIFORNIA VIN ROSÉ SEC Produced & bottled by Paul Masson Vineyards, Saratoga, California. Rating: 6. Distribution: A. Like so many vins rosés, this one has very little to offer besides its appearance in a wineglass. The aroma, while not terrible, gives the drinker nothing to look forward to, and makes me think of dank cellars. The taste is sweet, flat, and candylike, with a tinge of bitterness in the backtaste. Well chilled, these defects will diminish, but they'll never disappear totally. Price range: 25.4 oz, $2.15–2.39.

♉♉♉ MIRASSOU MONTEREY–SANTA CLARA PETITE ROSÉ Produced & bottled by Mirassou Vineyards, San Jose, California. Rating: 10. Distribution: B. This pink wine has a bright scarlet hue, and an engaging nose, clean and fresh and offering an interesting faint green weediness. The taste is also sprightly and fresh, semidry, showing a touch of complexity in the peppery fruit flavors. It's an enjoyable wine, well made, full of zest and energy, and if you can find a bottle, by all means try it. Price range: 25.6 oz, $2.75–3.19.

MOGEN DAVID CLASSIC ROSÉ Bottled by Mogen David Wine Corp., Chicago, Illinois. Rating: 7. Distribution: B. This wine has a very light color, almost more tawny than red. The nose shows some fruit and is by and large without defect. The taste is clean, but exceedingly sweet, without any redeeming acid to make the whole performance bearable. Maybe it might score with a very sweet dessert, but on the whole it's just too syrupy for me. Price range: 25.6 oz, $2.09–2.29.

CK MONDAVI CALIFORNIA SELECT VIN ROSÉ Made & bottled by C. Mondavi & Sons, St. Helena, California. Rating: 7+. Distribution: A. The wine is lovely and clear, darker than the average vin rosé. The nose is bashful, but what does present itself is floral and fruity. The fruit carries through into the mouth, where the sweetness overpowers the acid to some extent, but the result is still quite presentable. Price range: 25.4 oz, $1.59–1.89.

♈♈♈ ROBERT MONDAVI NAPA VALLEY GAMAY ROSÉ Produced & bottled by Robert Mondavi Winery, Oakville, California. Rating: 10. Distribution: A. The color is lipstick red. The nose is fruity and clean, with a faint tinge of brier. The taste is light hearted, simple, clean, lively, pleasantly fruity. It's a semidry wine with just enough sweetness and just enough acid to balance it nicely. I think you'll enjoy it. Price range: 25.4 oz, $2.75–3.19.

♈ MOTHER VINEYARD SOUTHERN SCUPPERNONG Made & bottled by Mother Vineyard Wine Co., Petersburg, Virginia. Rating: 8. Distribution: C. This is an interesting wine that might qualify to be served with dessert, or after dinner. It's a deep harvest orange, with a round, clean aroma that is very pleasing but seems to show more sweetness than fruit. The taste is sweet, thick, almost syrupy, an interesting, warm, smooth, fruity flavor with a faint spiciness in the background. If you've never tasted a wine made from scuppernong grapes, you ought to try it at least once, and this wine offers a pleasant way to do it. Price range: 25.6 oz, $1.69–1.99.

♈♈♈ NECTAROSE VIN ROSÉ DE FRANCE Produced & bottled by Maison J. H. Secrestat Aine, St. Hilaire-St. Florent, France. Rating: 10+. Distribution: A. Very few rosés show any complexity or character. This is one of the exceptions, but now that I've said that, don't look for *too* much complexity. The wine is a pale rose color, and the bouquet is lively, peppery, briery, and very pleasing. The taste is fruity and interesting, with a pleasant natural sweetness balanced in such a way that the result is an energetic and thoroughly enjoyable wine. Price range: 25 oz, $2.99–3.49.

OKAPI ROSÉ TABLE WINE   Produced & bottled by Sincomar, Casablanca, Morocco. Rating: 5+. Distribution: X. This wine is on the orange end of red-orange, almost tawny in its color. The nose is tolerable but baked, and the taste is sweet, syrupy, and full of that hot-weather flavor that often comes in grapes grown close to the equator. Price range: 24 oz, $1.39–1.69.

♀♀♀ ANGELO PAPAGNI CALIFORNIA MADERA ROSÉ Cellared & bottled by Papagni Vineyards, Madera, California. Rating: 10. Distribution: B. There is a note of formality, slightly hard and Chablis-like, in the nose of this clear, pink wine. There is a good measure of genial fruit in the taste, good acid balance, and a feeling of character. It has some sweetness, not too intense, and I think that you would do well to give it a try if you like pink wines. Price range: 25.6 oz, $2.20–2.59.

PEDRONCELLI SONOMA COUNTY ZINFANDEL ROSÉ Produced & bottled by J. Pedroncelli Winery, Geyserville, California. Rating: 7+. Distribution: B. The idea of a Zinfandel Rosé is a nice one, but Pedroncelli hasn't yet mastered it. The color is pale and washed out, the nose is thin and chemical. In the mouth the wine is thin, acidic, and lacking in character. Well chilled on a hot day it might save your life, but if it's not an emergency, you might look around for something more delectable. Price range: 25.6 oz, $2.00–2.49.

ΨΨΨ PETRI CALIFORNIA GRENACHE VIN ROSÉ   Produced & bottled by Petri Wineries, San Francisco, California. Rating: 11. Distribution: A. This is a find! Imagine, if you will, a fresh, inviting aroma full of flowers, fruit, sunshine and butterflies, and a taste a little on the sweet side but with fruit and the flavor of summer and outdoors, and then imagine it selling for the price of this wine . . . how would you like that? If I know you, you'd forgive the wine for being a little deficient in acid, and therefore a little flat, but you'd like it! Price range: 25.6 oz, $.99–1.39.

Ψ PETRI CALIFORNIA PINK CHABLIS   Produced & bottled by Petri Wineries, San Francisco, California. Rating: 8+. Distribution: A. There are touches of orange and tan in the color of this pink wine. The nose is right down the middle, shows a tiny bit of dankness, but is perfectly acceptable. There is some sweetness in the taste, but it's not overpowering. There's fruit aplenty, and every now and then, a faint reminder of the dank nose. Still, for what it is, a pink Chablis, it meets all the somewhat elastic qualifications. Price range: 25.6 oz, $.99–1.39.

ΨΨΨΨ SEBASTIANI NORTH COAST COUNTIES VIN ROSÉ Produced & bottled by Sebastiani Vineyards, Sonoma, California. Rating: 12. Distribution: A. Eureka! At last a vin rosé that has something to offer! Sebastiani's vin rosé is darker than most, but still very handsome. The bouquet offers fruit, spice, briers, excitement, and complexity. The mouth-feel is sprightly, the taste is interesting, fruity, refreshing. The whole thing seems to have a framework, a structure on which to hang all the parts of this well-integrated wine. I hope they sell it in your part of the world! Price range: 25.4 oz, $1.99–2.59.

♀ SEBASTIANI NORTHERN CALIFORNIA MOUNTAIN VIN ROSÉ Made & bottled by Sebastiani Vineyards, Sonoma, California. Rating: 8+. Distribution: A. The color is light scarlet. The nose is slightly floral, fresh, and inviting. The taste is semidry despite a touch of fruit sweetness, straightforward, a bit on the formal side, and with a moderate acid balance. Price range: 25.4 oz, $1.60–1.79.

♀♀♀ UVITA ROSÉ Produced & bottled by Dobbeletta & Cia., S.A., Mendoza, Argentina. Rating: 10. Distribution: C. Watch out for this rosé! It rates fairly high, but you may be disappointed if you're expecting just another sweet, inoffensive pink wine. The color is a clear, darkish pink. The nose is quite aromatic, interesting, pungent. The taste is rich with spice, briers, herbs, and fruit, and you may find that it has more character than you're looking for. Me, I like it, but it may be too intense and aggressive for you. So how do you find out? Try it. You won't be risking a great deal. Price range: 23.7 oz, $.99–1.39.

VINYA ROSÉ Produced & bottled by J. M. da Fonseca, Azeitão-Lisboa, Portugal. Rating: 7+. Distribution: C. The color is very light and on the tan side. The nose is pleasant enough, with some spiciness, but with an occasional whiff from the gas station. In the mouth it has some sweetness, some acid to balance it off, and the vulcanized note comes through again to keep this import from scoring any triumphs. Price range: 24 oz, $2.19–2.39.

♉♉ WENTE CALIFORNIA ROSÉ WENTE Produced & bottled by Wente Bros., Livermore, California. Rating: 9. Distribution: B. This rosé is a trace on the orange side, has an agreeable nose, and comes off semisweet, semidry in the mouth, which is not at all a bad sensation. It is refreshing, fruity, and has a slight feeling of austerity, which gives it a character that many vins rosés lack. All in all, it's a very nice wine for the right occasion. Price range: 25.6 oz, $2.15–2.59.

Sources of Supplies

Three places you can get corks, bottles, and all kinds of winemaking extracts and equipment, in person or by mail order:

Oak Barrel Winecraft
1201 University Avenue
Berkeley, CA 94702
(415) 849-0400

Wine and the People
907 University Avenue
Berkeley, CA 94702
(415) 549-1266

Wine Supply West
4324 Geary Boulevard
San Francisco, CA 94118
(415) 221-5137

Books on Making Your Own Wine

Some books to investigate in case you decide to make your own wine. Successful amateur winemakers of my acquaintance particularly recommend the first five.

The Art of Making Wine, by Stanley F. Anderson with Raymond Hull. Hawthorn, New York, 1970. Paperback.

Grapes into Wine, by Philip M. Wagner. Knopf, New York, 1974. Paperback.

Guidelines to Practical Winemaking, by Julius H. Fessler. Julius H. Fessler, 1965, P.O. Box 2842, Rockridge Station, Oakland, CA 94618. Paperback.

Progressive Winemaking, by Peter Duncan and Bryan Acton. Amateur Winemaker Publications, Andover, Hants., England, 1967. Paperback.

Technology of Winemaking, by Maynard Amerine. AVI Publishing Co., Westbury, Conn., 1971 (3rd edition). Hardcover.

American Wines and Winemaking, by Philip M. Wagner. Knopf, New York, 1970. Hardcover.

Country Wine Recipes, by Peter Brehm. Wine & the People, Berkeley, CA, 1972. Poster.

Easy Guide to Home-made Wine, by B. C. A. Turner. Mills & Boon, Toronto, 1968. Paperback.

First Steps in Winemaking, by C. J. J. Berry. Amateur Winemaker Publications, Andover, Hants., England, 1973. Paperback.

Home Winemaker's Handbook, by Walter S. Taylor and Richard P. Vine. Harper & Row, New York, 1968. Paperback.

Making Wines like Those You Buy, by Bryan Acton and Peter Duncan. Standard Press, Andover, Hants., England, 1973. Paperback.

Successful Winemaking at Home, by H. E. Bravery. ARC Books, New York, 1961. Paperback.

Winemaking with Concentrates, by Peter Duncan. Amateur Winemaker Publications, Andover, Hants., England, 1974. Paperback.

A Guide
to Bottle Sizes

New metric sizes	Metric sizes in fluid ounces	Closest present container, in fluid ounces		Number of bottles in a case
3.0 liters	101.4	Jeroboam	102.4	4
1.5 liters	50.7	Magnum	51.2	6
1.0 liter	33.8	Quart	32.0	12
750 milliliters	25.4	Fifth	25.6	12
375 milliliters	12.7	Tenth	12.8	24
187 milliliters	6.3	Split	6.4	48
100 milliliters	3.4	Miniature	2.0	60

Source: Federal Bureau of Alcohol, Tobacco & Firearms.